"The Object Les[sons] to magic: the b[ooks] and animate them with a rich history of invention, political struggle, science, and popular mythology. Filled with fascinating details and conveyed in sharp, accessible prose, the books make the everyday world come to life. Be warned: once you've read a few of these, you'll start walking around your house, picking up random objects, and musing aloud: 'I wonder what the story is behind this thing?'"

Steven Johnson, author of *Where Good Ideas Come From* and *How We Got to Now*

"Object Lessons describes themselves as 'short, beautiful books,' and to that, I'll say, amen. . . . If you read enough Object Lessons books, you'll fill your head with plenty of trivia to amaze and annoy your friends and loved ones— caution recommended on pontificating on the objects surrounding you. More importantly, though . . . they inspire us to take a second look at parts of the everyday that we've taken for granted. These are not so much lessons about the objects themselves, but opportunities for self-reflection and storytelling. They remind us that we are surrounded by a wondrous world, as long as we care to look."

John Warner, *The Chicago Tribune*

"In 1957 the French critic and semiotician Roland Barthes published *Mythologies*, a groundbreaking series of essays in which he analysed the popular culture of his day, from laundry detergent to the face of Greta Garbo, professional wrestling to the Citroën DS. This series of short books, Object Lessons, continues the tradition."

Melissa Harrison, *Financial Times*

"Though short, at roughly 25,000 words apiece, these books are anything but slight."

Marina Benjamin, *New Statesman*

"The Object Lessons project, edited by game theory legend Ian Bogost and cultural studies academic Christopher Schaberg, commissions short essays and small, beautiful books about everyday objects from shipping containers to toast. *The Atlantic* hosts a collection of 'mini object-lessons' . . . More substantive is Bloomsbury's collection of small, gorgeously designed books that delve into their subjects in much more depth."

Cory Doctorow, *Boing Boing*

" The joy of the series . . . lies in encountering the various turns through which each of their authors has been put by his or her object. The object predominates, sits squarely center stage, directs the action. The object decides the genre, the chronology, and the limits of the study. Accordingly, the author has to take her cue from the *thing* she chose or that chose her. The result is a wonderfully uneven series of books, each one a *thing* unto itself."

Julian Yates, *Los Angeles Review of Books*

" . . . edifying and entertaining . . . perfect for slipping in a pocket and pulling out when life is on hold."

Sarah Murdoch, *Toronto Star*

" . . . a sensibility somewhere between Roland Barthes and Wes Anderson."

Simon Reynolds, author of *Retromania: Pop Culture's Addiction to Its Own Past*

OBJECT LESSONS

A book series about the hidden lives of ordinary things.

Series Editors:

Ian Bogost and Christopher Schaberg

Advisory Board:

In association with

BOOKS IN THE SERIES

fake

KATI STEVENS

For Mary + Spencer,

Hope you enjoy the book.

♡, Kati

BLOOMSBURY ACADEMIC
NEW YORK · LONDON · OXFORD · NEW DELHI · SYDNEY

BLOOMSBURY ACADEMIC
Bloomsbury Publishing Inc
1385 Broadway, New York, NY 10018, USA
50 Bedford Square, London, WC1B 3DP, UK

BLOOMSBURY, BLOOMSBURY ACADEMIC and the Diana logo are trademarks
of Bloomsbury Publishing Plc

First published in the United States of America 2019

Cover design: Alice Marwick

Bloomsbury Publishing Inc does not have any control over, or responsibility for, any
third-party websites referred to or in this book. All internet addresses given in this
book were correct at the time of going to press. The author and publisher regret
any inconvenience caused if addresses have changed or sites have ceased to exist,
but can accept no responsibility for any such changes.

A catalog record for this book is available from the Library of Congress.

ISBN: PB: 978-1-5013-3813-7
ePDF: 978-1-5013-3815-1
eBook: 978-1-5013-3814-4

Series: Object Lessons

Typeset by Deanta Global Publishing Services, Chennai, India
Printed and bound in the United States of America

To find out more about our authors and books visit www.bloomsbury.com
and sign up for our newsletters.

For Grandma Nancy and Poppy

CONTENTS

1 THE START OF SOMETHING FAKE

I am sick of the word. Noun, adjective, and verb, overused and misused, in recent years fake's rap has gone from bad to downright malignant. All those members of the synonym posse that, since the beginning of the industrial revolution, have taken up some of the slack of the fake's burden are now in hiding, afraid of similar slander and blasphemy.

So close to meaning everything/nothing, the slur "fake" is now, ironically, the great, false equalizer. It is not another word for "fraud," but a meaning-stripped catchall epithet for the bad, the cheap, and the despised.

I want to give fake its clothes back. I want to take back the language around the fake, around what this word and its friends have meant historically, socioeconomically, and psychologically, and what they mean today. The bottom has fallen out for fake, but it has been a long time coming. For too long humans have given copies, imitations, substitutes, faux this and false that, short shrift. By putting the *ersatz* and the proxy in their proper places in the story of human invention and progress, perhaps people can finally separate these things from true "fakes" and understand the nature and power of such words and the objects they name.

Who's a phony?

Let's start with phony, the slur of choice for man among bildungsromen,* *The Catcher in the Rye*'s young Holden Caulfield. With the exception of his sister Phoebe, his dead younger brother Allie, and Jane Gallagher, the girl who got away, just about everyone and everything Holden encounters is deemed to be phony—his headmaster, his preparatory school, his ex-girlfriend, his favorite teacher, his screenwriter brother, his roommate, the prostitute he pays, the Edmont Hotel, the Seattle girls, Lillian Simmons, and, above all, himself.

Of all these characters and places, only the prostitute is trying to cheat Holden. With everyone else, the issue at hand is neither hypocrisy nor fraud, but what Holden—who knows little to nothing of their lives when they are not with him, of their relationships with their families and friends, and of their own internal narratives—perceives as inconsistency of logic or character. People and places do not measure up to an arbitrary standard Holden holds for the endlessly disappointing world around him, and he iconically and carelessly articulates that with the comforting insult "phony" in much the same way teenagers of the early twentieth

---

*The Internet says this is not the plural of bildungsroman. The Internet is fake.

century have thrown around "whatever." Haunted by the inability to be the person he wishes he was, Holden doesn't have the generosity of spirit to grant others ghosts because he is neither introspective nor forgiving with himself first. These people are not complex and flawed: they are simply phony.

Dating from the early 1900s, the word "phony" is believed to be an alteration of the British "fawney," the word for a gilded brass ring used in a confidence game called the "fawney rig."[1] In this game, the trickster drops a ring (or a purse with some seeming valuables in it) and runs to pick the item up at the same time as the poor sap who notices it on the ground. The trickster suggests the found treasure should be split between him and the aforementioned sap. Said sap, now convinced of the item's value, chooses instead to give the con artist some money in order to keep this object, that is, the fawney, all to himself. The object, of course, does not possess the value its new owner imagined—it's a phony.

As such, "phony" is actually the perfect word for Holden to glom onto because it is as much about his opinion of himself as it is of others. From the start, the nature of the phony has inspired no sympathy for the victim. The cheater, preying on that most human of weaknesses, greed, is not hustling a mark so much as finding a partner in mutual avarice. The cheater is simply more in tune with his venality, using his understanding of human psychology to acquire the cash his sharper intellect so richly deserves. Even if Holden didn't refer to himself as a phony as well, he'd still be damning himself by calling everyone around him the word.

Subconsciously he believes that phonies can smell the failings on him, that he deserves the terrible people he attracts.

Though the word "phony" came later, I imagine many contemporary readers of Thomas Bowdler, the nineteenth-century non-practicing British physician whose mission it was to produce volumes of Shakespeare fit "to be read aloud by a gentleman to a company of ladies," felt similarly swindled.*,2 But Bowdler did not see anything deceptive in himself or *The Family Shakspeare*, which altered or eliminated any language or plot point in Shakespeare's plays Bowdler deemed unwholesome—aka, all the fun bits. In fact, in his preface, Bowdler wrote,

> If a presumptuous artist should undertake to remove a supposed defect in the Transfiguration of Raphael, or in the Belvidere Apollo, and in making the attempt should injure one of those invaluable productions of art and genius, I should consider his name as deserving never to be mentioned, or mentioned only with him who set fire to the Temple of Diana.[3]

because he knew that neither paintings nor sculptures are in kind to books. To deface, or to so fail at restoration as to mar, Raphael's actual *Transfiguration,* a painting which currently resides in the Pinacoteca Vaticana in Vatican City, or the

---

*What lady wouldn't want to hear a single person read all the characters of a play out loud? I'm sure the Victorian and Edwardian eras were rife with Robin Williams' types waltzing into lady-packed salons to regale them with one-man readings of Hamlet void of epithets or insinuations of suicide.

Apollo Belvedere, a marble sculpture of the Greek god housed at the nearby Pio-Clementine Museum, would be definitively terrible; not burning a temple down bad, but horrific.

What Bowdler is doing, however, is not taking a chisel to someone else's sculpture, but building a replica with some tweaks of his own. He is not robbing the world of the original sculpture or changing the original to his own liking so that it is no longer the artist's work but his own, but rather iterating the work and providing a PG version of it for those with delicate sensibilities. Censorship disenfranchises artists when their names are placed on mauled versions of their work and the originals burnt, and it disenfranchises audiences deprived of context for different versions of a work, but *The Family Shakspeare* is guilty of neither. Without the preface or introduction, the bowdlerized Shakespeare would indeed be a fraud, a crime, because in that way it would be trying to pass itself off as unadulterated when it is not. Situationally, a bowdlerized copy (note that in the modern days a unit of a book is called a "copy") is not "real," per se, but neither is it a "phony" intending to trick unsuspecting readers—it's just lame.

And yet the English language does not look kindly on those who would dare "fub" with Shakespeare. Bowdler's name has travelled ignominiously down through the centuries as the verb "bowdlerize," meaning to excise material that is considered improper or offensive from media—usually books—resulting in the diminishment of the work. Ironically, the word is often used to describe acts of distortion and abridgement with which Bowdler would likely be uncomfortable having his name attached. While Bowdler's intent was never to maim Shakespeare or defraud his readers, he made of himself a model that others could willfully or accidentally misunderstand to serve their own interests. Surely Shakespeare, a neologist and dispenser of unkind but fitting fates, would have enjoyed Bowdler's comeuppance.

* * *

Once during a graduate school poetry class, I found myself arguing in defense of sincerity and honesty; exasperatingly, no one was on my side. While I actually championed naked candor, I think my fellow students and professor thought I was on the side of sentimentalism, the poetry of self-indulgence that tries "too hard" and thus can't be real. The truth of poetry, I learned, needs cover to survive the dash from one bombed-out stanza to the other. Otherwise it would be shot where it stands and left to bleed out behind a forgotten pile of rubble.

Art and literature, after all, are dependent upon metaphor, which is a cozy word for substitution, for proxy, for not the genuine article. A flower stands in for a vagina, a flower represents a vagina, but a flower is not a vagina. The fake vagina is art, profane and profound. The real vagina is biology, mere fact.

Facts too, expensive and unworked by human hands, make way for their metaphors. Cars replace horses, tofurkey replaces turkey, and texting replaces talking. Inventions steal the function and form of their forebears while making them more palatable to the needs and wants of progressive man. The ideas of real things are often more attractive than the actuality of them, so instead of animal skins we wear faux fur, plug in electric fireplaces, go to Epcot instead of Europe, and so on, for the most part without blinking an eye. Until we get confused and are no longer able to verbalize (to ourselves or to others) the difference between a real eye, a glass eye, glasses, contacts, and artificial visual stimuli, at which point we blink vigorously. At which point we tear our eyes out. At which point we stop seeing at all.

Language, like culture, is not the human species' bitch. They grow together, lichenous. What a person says, or writes, can rob another of her livelihood, tank an economy, start a war, end a war, cleave spouses together, rend them apart, render comfort, engender fear, establish law, commit fraud, form belief systems, encourage the taking up of arms, create, alter, destroy, rebuild. And this is what must be remembered about the dictionary, what must be remembered about so many historical documents that men turn into gospel, and what must be remembered about our own stupid, history-ignoring, history-repeating, history-worshipping, history-blaspheming selves: records set precedent because they are what have been done and what can be done, possibly what should be done, but are not one-way, one-lane paths with no on or off ramps. Context, circumstance, and situation—not only is no man an island, neither are events, objects, or even words.

Failure of communication and acknowledgment of context are at the heart of much of the story of fakes and their ilk. So consider this little book a plea for care and precision in how we think, talk, and write about this idea we have of what is inauthentic, proxy, substitute, unreal, and fake. We are taught that certain qualities are interchangeable, that these qualities mean certain things about product, places, and people, and we do not question the illogic that permeates this conversation. We don't want to think that all these times we called something we didn't like bad, and something bad fake, we have been making syllogistic errors that have taken over our worldview to such a degree that logical conversations are no longer possible and that our problems are no longer solvable because—real talk—all this time we have been perceiving them from a loaded angle and ascribing to them inaccurate basic elements.

If we aren't clear in our own minds about the nature of the so-called fakes of our past, present, and possible future, then we cannot be clear about truth and about reality, and we cannot choose our battles. We won't even know which side we're on.

2 THAT WHICH IS FAKE MAY NEVER DIE

If you would like to see a paradox in person, I highly recommend visiting your local Pottery Barn. Once inside you are bound to find yourself surrounded by flameless candles, their LED flickering powered by two AA batteries, standing safely inside hurricane lanterns.

Now the whole rationale of the hurricane rests in its name. When hard winds are a-blowing, a candle's flame is apt to be blown out or, worse, knocked over and light one's home on fire. High-sided glass hurricanes prevent everything, small breezes and violent tempests alike, from getting to the candle. But if a candle is electric and, therefore, does not possess a flame and can neither burn, melt, be extinguished by winds, nor set a building alight, why on Earth would someone put such a candle in a hurricane?

One could argue that this is done purely for display purposes—Pottery Barn and company can't very well be burning through all their candles with these demonstrations—which is a great argument until one realizes: both hurricanes AND their flameless candles are for sale at Pottery Barn. In fact, the different types of flameless candles you can buy at Pottery Barn far outnumber real wax candles. So why are there so many hurricanes and lanterns for sale if they have been rendered purposeless?

Consumers don't need the real thing, but they do need authenticity from the scenarios in which they place themselves. So-called fake things demand support systems. Fake flowers get real clay pots and vases; fake fruit real bowls. When imitation objects are coupled with their real counterparts, their natural settings, it is not out of a need to fool guests or even the hosts. Rather, people are:

1   Telling the thing that is not quite the thing, "Welcome. You are equal to what you ape. I do not consider you less than."

2   Telling themselves that the material substance may not be organic, but domestication started that process millennia ago, and there's just no turning back now. The settings in which natural things are placed are just as unnatural as the manufacturing of electric or plastic replicas—and yet far more accepted.

For millennia mankind has been incrementally improving upon what nature can provide in order to make itself safer, warmer, and healthier. The house was likely not the first artificial thing, but it certainly has been the most important.

Dissatisfied by the less-than-optimal shelters of trees and caves, man took the skins and bones of a mammoth and made tents, rejecting the limits of nature no less definitively than Adam and Eve. Later, man improved upon tents with mud brick houses. Log cabins, stone manors, and split-level ranches with fiberglass insulation between the plaster walls and vinyl siding have followed, offering greater space and protection from heat and predators that naturally occurring shelters could not.

The human species brought the outside inside and transformed it to fit. She* who had brought heat from the sun down to earth in the form of fire now cast it into a hearth, controlled its size with torches and candles, and at last converted it into electric light. She brought the forest and the rivers inside. She brought the animals in. None of it looked the same as it did out there, but it suited her better. And when she dared leave her home, she still carried shelter with her. She had her clothes.

Many, many years ago, long before you or I or anyone we have met was born, a Neanderthal hunter brought home a bison for his daughter to skin and throw on the fire. And this young woman, upon finishing her duties, instead of tossing the hide as all had done before, dared her younger sister to put on the hide and pretend to be a bison. The younger

---

*I find rage attacks brought on by pronoun choice are easily cured by sitting upside-down on one's couch and humming one's favorite The Who song.

sister, like younger sisters everywhere, wanted to impress her sibling and so donned the fur. Yes, it smelled terrible, and, yes, she was covered with fluids, but, boy, if she wasn't warm.

And so was born the custom of wearing clothing made out of animals' skins and, more specifically, furs. No one knows exactly when this fashion choice began, but the Armenians had leather shoes 3,500 years before Jesus was walking around barefoot for no good reason. We do know, however, when man started to leave his furry friends alone and don petroleum-based imitations instead: the early twentieth century, courtesy of two world wars.

While people had been wearing flax and hemp, cotton and silk as well in the interim, it was the minute prehistoric man "discarded the pelt of skins"[1] for woven wool that the textile industry began. Problem is people didn't actually "discard" them so much as expand their wardrobes for reasons ranging from fashion to cost, and somewhere along the way, probably sometime after man decimated a great number of the world's biggest fur providers, fur became rare, expensive, and so a status symbol, and so fashionable, desirable.

If human ingenuity weren't what it is, this could have remained the case, but when something in America becomes fashionable and desirable, companies rise to meet the demand and, often enough, kill the status symbol that teed off the FOMO* in the first place.

---

*Fear of missing out.

Fakes in the fur industry had been mentioned in US newspapers as early as 1904. In the *Cecil Whig*, reports out of Russia claimed that the fur business was in jeopardy because "a common hare skin can be manufactured to represent a valuable dark brown fox, and to such perfection that only an expert may discover the difference,"[2] and as a result the rare and more valuable animals were now being priced out.

From 1919 to 1928, however, the American government imposed a 10 percent tax on all fur[3] as one of several new taxes to fund the war effort. From that point on fur, regardless of the animal it came from, was just too expensive for the common woman, and the fashion started to reflect the times by employing fur only in trims or not at all. A writer for the *Evening Star* in 1920 wrote that the truly great furs of the past, such as mink and seal, were now spoken of as being as covetable and out of reach as "diamond tiaras and private yachts."[4]

First introduced in 1929, "real" fake fur—fake fur that openly self-identified as fake—was not made out of animals at all, but was a pile fabric, a type of textile in which upright loops or strands of yarn of various knot densities are attached to a backing. Thanks to a second fur-trade-disrupting World War, development of synthetic fabrics made non-animal fake fur available to the masses, and by the time fake fur was finally commercially available in the 1950s[*] both silks and

---

[*] Which means that all teddy bears made before that were terrifying monsters? Logical question, and the answer is . . . not all, but some. Mohair

acrylic fibers were capable of pulling off fur imitations of just about any animal the fashion industry could imagine.

Though fake fur has waxed and waned in popularity in the eyes of both designers and consumers since then, until recently fake fur has always had the support of animal-rights activists. Then something very strange happened.

In the autumn of 2013, having lab-tested several different styles of Nicole Lee handbags from Kohls.com advertised as featuring "faux-fur" trim, Humane Society investigators determined the fur to not be synthetic at all, but from a rabbit.[5] Less than a year later the Humane Society found, once again, that a Kohl's product's fake fur wasn't genuinely fake—this time the men's R&O Hooded Parka's "faux-fur trim" turning out to be made of raccoon dog fur.[6]

Kohl's was not alone. In the same year The Neiman Marcus Group Inc., DrJays.com Inc., and Eminent Inc., doing business as Revolve Clothing, all settled Federal Trade Commission charges that their products contained real fur while being marketed as containing only "faux fur."

Although one could posit that economics is to explain for the switch—real fur, especially that from animals that are either plentiful or undesirable, may be cheaper than synthetic fibers—plenty of other examples of goods not falling in

---

from long-haired goats was used sometimes, so one could cuddle in bear-form the warm, scratchy hair of animals that were still living continents away. Alpaca teddy bears, on the other hand, were basically taxidermy with a twist, alpaca skins molded into the shape of another animal.

the traditional good-real-expensive and bad-fake-cheap categories exist, and not all of them are quite so explicable.

In 2017, for instance, Balenciaga released a large blue $2,145 purse that strongly resembled Swedish furniture behemoth Ikea's 99-cent "FRAKTA" shopping bag. The famous FRAKTA bag is entirely made of polypropylene, while the Balenciaga leather "Arena Extra-Large Shopper Tote Bag" is lined with black fabric and made in Italy. The news outlets mocked Balenciaga and Barney's, the department store where the bag was being sold, while Ikea took the media circus in stride, telling *TODAY*, "We are deeply flattered that the Balenciaga tote bag resembles the Ikea iconic sustainable blue bag for 99 cents. Nothing beats the versatility of a great big blue bag."[7]

In this circumstance, the cheap plastic object came first, and it was the fancy, pricier object that came afterward. No one would ever refer to a Balenciaga as a "fake" or a "knockoff," and yet by modern standards the terminology would apply. Online harassment and media jesting disappeared quickly, and Balenciaga never put out a statement about the bag. Whether the bag's design imitation was intentional or accidental, no one seemed to care. If the copy or copied had been a mid-price bag, would things have been different? Was the absurdity of the price differentials—the super cheap item versus its prohibitively expensive counterpart—so great that it would defy any suggestion of bad faith? Their customers could not be the same; the materials were clearly night and day; rationalization, rationalization.

Whether accidental, purposeful, or inevitable, imitation objects can have purpose and good to them—they can provide approximately equal goods or services to those who can't afford or don't have access to the "real" thing; they can help protect limited resources, like endangered species, and reduce waste; they can be safer, healthier, and in many other ways preferable to the original; apparently they can also give people with too much money and cheap taste a way of resolving their paradoxical circumstances— it all depends on the object and the imitation. How people react to imitation objects, however, is often distinct from the purpose of the imitation. Instead, it is how the market, media, and (occasionally) the law respond to such imitation objects, whether with amusement, distress, or condemnation, that directs the public's opinion and interaction.

* * *

Fashion isn't the only retail sector where what's real and what's worth purchasing become matters of cultural identification and social pressure. In his essay for themillions.com about how and why print literary journals could and should be saved, *Barrelhouse Magazine*'s non-fiction editor Tom McAllister isn't satisfied by pro-"real" books people's fetishization of physical journals. Noting how people express their love of the olfactory and physical qualities of paper, McAllister writes, "There has to be more than the smell of the pages or the tactile pleasure of holding a book. I already own lots of books. Why do I need to feel or smell more of them?"[8]

My youngest sister Michelle is one of those book "purists" who put a high value on tangibility. She refuses to buy an e-reader, and, meanwhile, is regularly forced to cull her untenable pile of physical books. A principle is at hand here, but it is a vague one that is in turn about the danger e-readers pose to the publishing industry and the future of books (e-readers are more and more seen as supplementary rather than replacements for physical books, though critics still rarely seem to note that e-readers also increase access to literature) and a position stemming from that inherent, hard-to-admit human prejudice toward technology—a self-preservation mechanism humans should hope never to lose, but also one they should recognize the nature of within themselves—rather than anything to do with the actual form and function of books.

In truth there is a greater disparity between privately owned books and library books than between physical books and their digital counterparts. I recently borrowed a marginalia-riddled copy of Jean Baudrillard's *Simulacra and Simulation* from the American University library through a friend. The marginalia were not in the book Baudrillard wrote, nor in the book the University of Michigan published, but added by different AU students over the years. The marginalia, living parts of the book, are now a fundamental part of how anyone who reads this copy experiences it. Other libraries bear different marginalia, missing pages, underlinings, and so on.

If I were to add more marginalia to this book or erase what already exists, the *Simulacra* the next person reads would be different from the one that I am reading.

A book happens many times to many people, never in the same way, never the same book. Readers have heard this before and half-believed it, but the inverse is true too—readers happen to books. While what each person takes from a book is different, we also shape them in our own image and transform them by excerpting them, recommending them, ignoring them, Bowdlerizing them, misinterpreting them, and savaging them. We purchase them and never read them, lend them to friends, give them as gifts, assign them in classes, sell them at stores. We do this for all objects—shape them by our interactions, thus removing any falseness they could possibly have. An object in the world, forced into action and interaction, loses any innate base value, but becomes a relationship. Objects happen to people, people happen to objects, and each to themselves.

With the exception of objects that are lying to consumers—fraudulent objects—most things we deem "fake" do what they are supposed to do. Maybe not as well, maybe not with the same aesthetic or emotional experience as the originals, but they still fulfill their requisite functions. As much as I adore books and magazines as bodies, their main purpose is to carry a story from writer to reader, not to be palpably pulpable. Electronic devices in no way sabotage that primary directive. They are the inverse of hurricanes for electric candles—artificial support systems for real things.

Fakeness does exist in the instances mentioned earlier, though, and does so in a way that is unique and viral, that has metastasized so far from fraud, purposeless yet voracious, that it has painted the objects in pure paradox. It is not the electric candle that is fake, but the hurricane that houses it; it is not the faux fur that is fake, but the fake faux fur.

The fakeness or realness of an object, like its value, comes not just from its actual substance but from human perception. As with the uncertainty principle, it is interaction and engagement with an object that has power and effect, not the object as unobserved, locked away, discrete. And, when we name an object a fake, we are not truly naming the object but the spaces between it and what came before, it and society, it and ourselves.

3 QUORN FOR LUNCH; OREOS FOR DESSERT

When Michelle was nine years old and I was fifteen, my mom dragged us to something called the Home Show at the Hartford Civic Center (now the XL Center) in Connecticut. In one of the trailers on the show floor Michelle noticed a bowl of fruit. Thinking that the fruit was real and free for public consumption, Michelle grabbed one of the green apples and took a bite.

It took her until the second bite to realize it was foam, and then, because my middle sister Allison and I were making fun of her, she obstinately took a third bite as well.

She sure showed us.

For years when I heard or read the term "fake food," my first thoughts were always of my little sister consuming half of a realistic-looking, waxed, decorative trailer apple. But what people term as "fake food" covers a large swath of disparate things—plastic fruit, certainly, but also heavily processed "junk" foods, *ersatz* food, food substitutes, chemically manufactured foods, other so-called analogues, and meat grown in a lab.

In the proto days of humanity man survived on what he could tear from the ground, shake from branches, and stone to death. Change was slow. Though *Homo sapiens* were collecting and cooking shellfish as early as 164,000 years ago, there is no proof modern humans were making tools specifically for fishing[1] until 90,000 years ago. If it took man that many millennia to figure out fishing, it's no wonder the first "processed food"—unleavened bread—doesn't show up in the archaeological record until 30,000 years ago, or that no one seems to have been fermenting alcohol until the Chinese did it with rice around 7000 BCE. Even then the processed food craze didn't really get rolling (albeit slowly) until olive oil and leavened bread showed up sometime between 4500 and 3500 BCE, the earliest evidence of beer appearing around the same time in Mesopotamia. Palm oil and cheese arrived around 3000 BCE, and, now possessing all the ingredients to make a kick-ass grilled cheese sandwich, apron-festooned man has never looked back.

If you have read a fitness or health magazine in the last few decades, then you have probably come across the idea of "processed food" being less-than-real food, absent the proviso that approximately 70 percent of all food is processed and much of what isn't you process yourself at home through baking, cooking, or otherwise preparing your snacks and meals. Basically, unless you're eating a raw fruit or vegetable, the food you eat is processed, and that in of itself doesn't make it less real, nor does it necessarily make the food unhealthy. If the human species has been processing food for thousands of years and processed foods are so much a part of our history—heck, even our evolution—haven't they earned the right to be called "real"?

I am not disputing that the more processed food is the less it resembles anything in nature. When it comes to "ultra-processed" food, the problem is typically augmented by a destruction of nutrients and the incorporation of enough unhealthy additives to keep man in fat pants for the rest of his shortened life. Do some processed foods' proven addictive and fattening qualities make them fake? For a quick baseline check let's take a glance at the consummate junk food of our time, the Oreo cookie.

Oreos (not Birthday Cake Oreos or Candy Corn Oreos or Peanut Butter Oreos or Cookie Dough Oreos or Red Velvet or Blueberry Pie Oreos, just standard boring old classic Oreos) are made up of the following ingredients:

- Unbleached enriched flour (wheat flour, niacin, reduced iron, thiamine mononitrate {B1}, riboflavin {B2}, and folic acid)
- Sugar
- Palm and/or canola oil
- Cocoa (processed with alkali)
- High fructose corn syrup

- Leavening (baking soda and/or calcium phosphate)
- Cornstarch
- Salt
- Soy lecithin
- Vanillin
- Chocolate

Which of these are the "fake" ingredients, and which of these are the ingredients that are unhealthy for you, and which of these are the ingredients derived from slave labor, and which of these are the ingredients harvested through environmentally hostile practices? If the creation of an ultra-processed food leaves an unflattering mark on the world, there is nothing fake about it—it is altogether too real.

Many of the ingredients listed may be things that shouldn't be made or considered fit for human consumption. When put together, these ingredients produce an arguably tasty cookie that, if eaten in a certain quantity over a certain period of time, equally arguably may lead to the deterioration of one's health; those ingredients, however, do not produce a lethal poison or something that is non-comestible. The cookie is not claiming to be anything it is not. It is not trying to pull a fast one on us. As such, Oreos may be classified as junk food, but they can't be classified as fake food. They are (a) edible and (b) up front about what they are.

The same, alas, cannot be said for other categories of fake food.

That red letter "E"

Memory is hardly reliable, but when I was younger it seemed like Maine was chock-full of cute roadside restaurants operating out of houses. All of them served pie, and my grandmother nearly always allowed us to order dessert when we stopped at one for lunch. One summer a few years before the plastic apple incident, my grandmother took us kids to a place that had something called Tollhouse Pie on the menu. I knew what Tollhouse meant—chocolate chip cookies. It sounded like a combination of my two favorite desserts, so I was extremely disappointed when the dessert that came out was filled with nuts and hard as a brick. I mashed the whipped cream topping into the pie to see if that would help. It did not. Then, when Michelle, the same sister who ate the foam apple, went to the bathroom, I had a brilliant idea. With Allison's support I put everything that was on the table into the pie and whipped cream mixture—various beverages, salt, pepper, Tabasco sauce, ketchup, maple syrup, and other myriad scraps from our lunch—and blended it in so Michelle wouldn't be able to tell we had done anything untoward to the pie other than mashing it. When she came out of the bathroom, I offered her my mutilated dessert and watched in wonder as she ate the whole thing without so much as a grimace.

The only difference between me and the purveyors of tainted food is that I wanted to be caught. I wanted Michelle to notice the disgusting elements of the repulsive concoction and spit it out. In my case the contamination was not sufficient to stop my sister from housing that pie. Typically for purveyors of fraudulent food this would have been a win because they don't want to be found out, but for every rule there is an exception beyond sibling-on-sibling pranks—in this case, war, where *ersatz* goods weren't simply accepted but critical to everyday survival.

Though *ersatz* is but the German word for substitute or replacement, to the English-speaking mind *ersatz* connotes goods that have been adulterated with ingredients that don't belong and are perceived as inferior, particularly in food, which is probably why Mary Elizabeth Massey called her 1952 book about privations in the South during the American Civil War *Ersatz in the Confederacy: Shortages and Substitutes on the Southern Homefront.*

An import-heavy society must be careful about going to war. In the mid-nineteenth century the Confederacy had a monopoly on cotton and had failed to sufficiently diversify into any other crop or industry. As hostilities commenced, necessary commodities like "hay, meat, horses, butter, cheese, clothing, shoes, beverages, paper, candles, oil, kerosene, glass, rope, cordage, soap, and starch" suddenly vanished from stores. Writing not long after the Second World War, Massey realized that the shortages and substitutions that characterized Confederacy home life would be recognizable to all Americans who had gone through the War years.

When wars cause shortages of food (due to embargoes, blockades, loss of manpower, destruction of agriculture, etc.[2]), entrepreneurs have two options: they can get into the smuggling business, or they can get in the *ersatz* business. Smuggling is dangerous, and, especially when customers are too poor to pay the high prices that make smuggling worthwhile, it may be safer and more economically viable for the entrepreneur to engage in *ersatz* production.

When people are starving, they will eat anything—"So bad did the situation become in some [Confederate] cities that the inhabitants were seen eating the refuse from garbage cans"[3]—but what makes *ersatz* food unique is that it is doing its damnedest to provide a psychological and sociological benefit via suspension of disbelief. After all, things can't be so bad if you can still have "oysters":

Recipe for "Artificial Oysters" from a cookbook of the time:

> Take young green corn, grate it in a dish; to one pint of this add one egg, well beaten, a small teacup of flour, two or three tablespoonfuls of butter, some salt and pepper, mix them all together.
>
> A tablespoonful of the batter will make the size of an oyster. Fry them light brown, and when done butter them. Cream if it can be procured is better.[4]

With a little imagination and a whole lot of patriotism, all things were possible. Even an "Apple Pie without Apples" could be had with nothing more than a bowl of crackers, tartaric acid, butter, "a very little nutmeg,"[5] and some serious Southern mettle.

A key element of such self-delusion is how substitute foodstuffs are named. To make *ersatz* food more palatable to their minds if not their tongues, Southerners often added patriotic monikers "Rebel," "Stonewall," "Jackson," "Jeff Davis," "Beauregard," and, unsurprisingly, "Confederate" to their groceries and recipes. As Cameron C. Nickels writes in *Civil War Humor*, "Confederate" had a greater duty beyond *ersatz* food. "The operative word in the Confederacy was 'substitute,' and Confederate became a synonym for that, as in 'Confederate coffee,' 'Confederate tea,' 'Confederate dresses,' and 'Confederate beer.'"[6]

This propagandizing of food was not only not limited to the Civil War, but in other wars taken to value judgment extremes directly opposite to those in peacetime. For example, citizens who ate "real food" during wartime were often derided as less patriotic than others. During the First World War an acting FDA* administrator in Oregon shamed citizens who bought Victory Bread, which contained only 35 percent wheat substitutes, as being 15 percent less patriotic, mathematically, than those who ate War Bread, which contained 40 percent wheat substitutes.[7]

While most *ersatz* foods die out with the ends of war, desperation regularly leads to innovation. Peanuts were not

---

*Food and Drug Administration.

eaten regularly in the United States until the Civil War made them a substitute for meat. Sunflower seed oil substituted for olive oil[8] and continues to be available as a cheaper alternative on grocery store shelves. With the sugar shortage, plentiful sorghum took its place,[9] and, as of 2014, according to data from the Food and Agriculture Organization of the United Nations, the United States was the top producer of sorghum in the world. And, obviously, if you go to the grocery store, the bread aisle offers plenty of different kinds of bread other than white bread, including ones that would have been treated as lesser wartime provisions in the early part of the twentieth century.

When it comes to coffee, however, no amount of faith in the cause seems to make substitutes go down smoothly. Though the *Southern Banner* published an 1863 recipe from a Mr. Archer Griffeth of Alabama for making coffee out of okra seed,[10] in 1865 the newspaper admitted that "for the stimulating property to which both tea and coffee owe their chief value, there is unfortunately no substitute; the best we can do is to dilute the little stocks which still remain, and cheat the palate, if we cannot deceive the nerves."[11]

While many may agree on the latter sentiment, as long as there have been coffee drinkers there have been people so dependent upon the beverage that they will try anything to get an approximate fix when faced with a shortage. Between the sixteenth and nineteenth centuries, British sailors were making something called "Scotch coffee" by dissolving burnt bread in hot water and adding some sugar.[12] By the end of the

Civil War, nothing had more substitutes than coffee. Though rye and okra seed proved the most popular, attempts were made with "acorns, dandelion roots, sugar cane, parched rice, cotton seed, sorghum molasses, English peas, peanuts, wheat, and beans."[13] While Union soldiers had a daily allotment of "one-tenth of a pound of green coffee beans,"[14] desperate Confederate soldiers had little choice but to go cold turkey or "take sound ripe acorns, wash them while in the shell, dry them, and parch until they open, take the shell off, roast with a little bacon fat,"[15] close their eyes, and pray for courage.

These vile nineteenth-century concoctions never made the cut, but experimentation in coffee alternatives, and how to convince the public of their worth, continued into the twentieth century and for a time did great business. C. W. Post, the man behind the Post Cereal Company, ran a smart smear campaign against coffee, exaggerating and inventing physical side effects caused by the caffeine in coffee—something consumers need not fear in his Postum, an instant type of caffeine-free coffee substitute made from roasted wheat bran, wheat, and molasses.

From a 1901 ad:

I would not give one cup of Postum for all the coffee that grows in Central America, not only as a drink, but for what it has done for my health.

Richard Wilhelm, 823 E. Main st., and his wife both suffered from dyspepsia, but were cured by quitting coffee and using Postum Food Coffee.

James Neukamp, a grocer on East Fulton st., had liver complaint. He has been greatly benefited by leaving off coffee and taking Postum.[16]

With the success of Postum came copycats, so in the same ads that were scaring people off coffee, Post turned his advertising against his own imitators, calling their product "a cheap, low grade adulterated coffee"[17] and saying that "a counterfeiter cares little what goes into a customer's stomach."[18]

Incidentally, Postum's success came during the heyday of American muckraking. If you have seen the Academy Award–winning film *It Happened One Night*, then you know the work of Samuel Hopkins Adams, upon whose 1933 short story "Night Bus" the plot of the movie is based. Before he got into fiction, Adams day-jobbed as a journalist, first at the *New York Sun*, then at *McClure's Magazine* where he began writing articles on public health in the United States. In his 1905 to 1906 series for *Collier's Weekly*, "The Great American Fraud," Adams stood up, perhaps irascibly, for his "Gullible America" whose government wasn't doing enough to protect consumers from fraudulent patent-medicine makers. In the first installment of the series, Adams noted specifically that the Patent Office, by issuing trade-mark registration "without inquiry into the nature of the article,"[19] and the Post Office, by permitting the distribution of "advertising and circular statements . . . materially and substantially false"[20] through the mail, were complicit in the defrauding of the American people.

The government was not alone. In the sixth installment Adams called out an accomplice closer to home—the print media:

Advertising and testimonials are respectively the aggressive and defensive forces of the Great American Fraud. Without the columns of the newspapers and magazines wherein to exploit themselves, a great majority of the patent medicines would peacefully and blessedly fade out of existence.

Study the medicine advertising in your morning paper, and you will find yourself in a veritable goblin-realm of fakery, peopled with monstrous myths.[21]

When your reporter accuses newspapers and magazines of impropriety within the confines of your own publication, you better have clean hands yourself. Regrettably, *Collier's* did not, having published Post's ads, which, "invariably touted medicinal cures."[22] In order not to be hypocritical, *Collier's* not only stopped running Post's ads, but in 1907 denounced Post's claims that Grape-Nuts was a cure for appendicitis.

Post took the potshot and declared war, filling the pages of less discerning papers with an article-advertisement campaign under the headline "The 'Yell-Oh' Man And One of His Ways"[23] with this fantastic paragraph:

We had understood that the editor of "Collier's" was a wild cat of the Sinclair "jungle bungle" type, a person with curdled gray matter but it seems strange that the owners would descend to using their editorial columns, yellow as they are, for such rank out and out falsehoods.

Collier's response? A libel suit. I know I'm really spending a lot of time on this story, but you have purchased this book and it would be a crime to leave this crazy battle without getting to the best part. Post, instead of shutting up about Collier's until their suit went to court, almost immediately put out even MORE incendiary material, moving from carpet bombing to thermonuclear warfare with more article-ads under the headline—and I'm not joking—"'Boo-hoo' Shouts a Spanked Baby,"[24] where unnamed religious sources were quoted accusing *Collier's* of an "utmost disregard for the facts" and saying the magazine "cries and boo hoos like a spanked baby and wants $750,000.00 to soothe its tender, lacerated feelings."

Post lost the suit. Though the verdict was eventually reversed, Postum's campaign style changed course as a result with ads moderating the general wellness experienced by consumers and insinuating at caffeine's dangers without getting into legally actionable specifics.

More importantly, at the same time all this was happening, Dr. Harvey Wiley at the Chemistry Bureau was spearheading the passage of the Pure Food and Drug Act, and his main concerns were Post related: adulteration and mislabeling. These are still the cornerstones of the act, though for Wiley, whether tainted food and drugs might have deleterious effects on consumers was almost beside the point. "The real evil of food adulteration," he wrote, "is deception of the consumer." For the government fake food, or not-pure food, was ultimately not a matter of the ingredients of Postum coffee, Raisin Bran, or any other foodstuffs being peddled to the American consumer, but rather the honesty of manufacturers and salesmen.

It's been over 110 years since the passage of the Pure Food and Drug Act in America, and since then not only have there been the aforementioned World Wars, accompanied by rationing and *ersatz* foods, but also a boom in imported foods, leaps and bounds in genetic engineering, and the advent of supermarkets vast enough to house multiple 747s. Throughout this evolution in the way humans eat, the common anxiety goes back to this matter of truth in advertising. The less consumers know about their food, the more they may act as anyone might when faced with a life's necessity playing coy: with suspicion. Only knowledge can allay their fears and subdue their anger, and more than just knowledge of a food's ingredients and calories. Today wary consumers demand to know where the food comes from, under what conditions it lived and died and was transported to us, what chemicals and allergens it has encountered along the way, whether the people who grew and harvested or killed our food were paid well if they were paid at all, what the food means to its local environment and economy as well as the world's, how long it has been waiting for us to purchase it, and whether it might eventually cause cancer or some other illness. Written out like that, it seems like a lot to ask, but is it too much to expect of food producers and distributors that the food we buy be that which they claim it to be—that what we eat be what we want to eat, need to eat, should eat, or thought we were eating if we weren't too tired to think about it too much in the first place.

Transparency then is the surprise silver lining about the cheap junk processed foods that list all their artificial, horrible ingredients. The food that we should worry about deceiving us is typically that which swears up and down it is not only organic, but cheap, nutritious, and tasty as well. We want everything, so we are told we can have everything, and, if we do look that gift horse in the mouth, we may come to find out it was actually donkey all along.

Though I am inclined to share Dr. Wiley's opinion that the only "real" fake food is food that claims to be X and is actually Y, I do think there are degrees of lying. Sometimes food that claims to be X isn't Y either, but 14—in other words, not food at all, which can be dangerous. Should "Parmesan" containing wood pulp filler[25] not be considered worse than honey diluted by corn syrup or so-called Kobe beef that's not actually Kobe beef, but still meat from a cow? And if either of these things were in fact contaminated with or entirely made from a lethal or sickening non-food (I know what you're going to say about corn syrup, but I'm talking along the lines of the 2008 Chinese milk scandal in which infant formula was tainted with melamine and resulted in infant deaths), why do all these items exist on the same spectrum known as "fake" when some are so "fake" as to be fatal?

If you want to eat Kobe beef and be certain you truly are eating Kobe beef, which is as regulated by Japan as cheese is by Italians and wine is by the French, as of July 2017 there were only sixteen licensed US distributors of Kobe beef, but you wouldn't know it because restaurants aren't held to the same federal labeling standards as products in stores and can call any hunk of cow they throw on your plate Kobe. Though some restaurants may be required to divulge calorie counts or allergens, many are still free to call the fish on their menu an entirely different name from what appears on your plate. And even if restaurateurs and chefs are not consciously deceiving customers, the manufacturers, distributors, and/ or importers further up the food chain (pun intended) are, and they are doing so about nearly everything we eat, from seafood and beef to honey and cheese to wine and chocolate.

Cali-Quorn-Ication

I first met Quorn in New York City. The summer after graduation I was subletting a floor of a Harlem brownstone with a friend from college named Smita. Smita lustered—her hair, her skin, her eyes, not so much her feet because she had battered runner toes, but every other part of her body as well as her mind. I too wanted to shimmer and radiate and look like I had been born with conditioner in my veins, so I pretended not to know about genetics and paid attention to her lifestyle choices, adopting them whenever possible, but mostly just marveling.[*]

It was here in this brownstone, in our common refrigerator, that I one day found Smita's Quorn nuggets. They're meatless, she said, as if I had forgotten she was a vegetarian. I had so many questions about these bite-sized paradoxes. Were they made out of vegetables like some burgers? Why didn't she just eat mushrooms in their natural spongiform state[†]instead of forcing them into nugget form? Turns out even shiny people have cravings for crap, same as you and me, and America has found a way to cater to them with so-called healthy junk food—Wheat Thins, kettle corn,

---

[*]I did, however, not eat egg yolks for seven years because of Smita. Studies now suggest this probably did me zero good in the long run.

[†]Just a quick tangent. Did you know there's a mushroom that looks just like a sponge that's actually called *spongiform squarepantsii*, aka the SpongeBob SquarePants mushroom? The species doesn't live in a pineapple under the sea but rather in the jungles of Malaysian Borneo and was named by American mycologists Dennis E. Desjardin, Kabir Peay, and Thomas Bruns in 2011, presumably to make me the happiest person on the planet. Yes, we are naming an actual sponge after an animated sponge—another foray into the hyper-real—but clearly an appreciation for a gleefully absurd cartoon did not prevent these young men from becoming scientists and successful ones at that. Our ancestors paid homage to gods who were figments of their imaginations—hell, based their whole lives and deaths around invented vengeful personifications of weather, climate, and basic animal flaws like greed and the desire to group. Would that they had been so tongue-in-cheek in their references.

sweet potato fries, trail mix, yogurt. She had no qualms with the nugget aspect of the nugget, she said, just the chicken.

Then she told me her Quorn nuggets were actually made of slime mold.

The chicken nugget, the first nugget, so often maligned as being meat no longer identifiable as meat, pink goo, and a nutritional abomination, now finds itself a progenitor of fake healthy foods, wannabe kid bait on the outside, textured vegetable protein, soy protein, or mycoprotein within. Second-order derivatives billing themselves as better for you than the first-order fakes, "chick'n" nuggets still participate in the junk food culture at which they sneer yet earn themselves a pass. Smita was right. It's the nugget that matters, not its content, the burger not the meat. The shape or form that consumers disdain is also what they find so addicting. Rather than kicking their bad habit, they allow manufacturers to futz with the product until it is no longer a guilty pleasure, so much as the shadow of one. With less pleasure, after all, comes less guilt.

Man is consistently inconsistent in his love of futzing and never more so than when it comes to genetically modified organisms, or GMOs. Though selective breeding helped create the hunt-for-sport-not-to-prevent-starvation world he lives in today, genetic modification as accomplished by industry does not sit as well with him. When California wanted to require GMO labeling, I voted against the measure because, in all the anti-Monsanto vitriol, there was no clear statement of what would be considered a GMO and what information would be available in the label. Distrust for what goes on in labs is interesting because it tends to pick and choose what areas are dangerous or messing with God and which are giving us cell phones and curing diseases. GMO labeling bills are often fought against because there is a sense that, if people see that the food they plan to purchase has been modified or engineered, if they only have the knowledge they seek (a single word or phrase on a package or sticker), but not all the extra factors required to make fully informed choices, then they will automatically equate GMO with bad (unnatural, inorganic, and/or unsafe) and thus not consume it.

Of course, there are legitimate concerns that, with the Frankensteining of food, religious people may believe they are endangering their souls by consuming food without all the information. Specifically, genetic engineering can complicate matters because animal DNA can be implanted in fruits and vegetables: Muslims, Hindus, Jews, vegetarians, and other people with belief systems that preclude the consumption of various animals may feel that such fruits and vegetables are no longer permissible for them to eat. Regardless of whether scientists or businesses feel such a threshold has been reached, that kind of information needs to be provided. Omission of *desired* information about what is in food can be considered lying, and it's been happening for far longer than genetic engineering has been around.

In 2002, for example, McDonald's agreed to donate $10 million to Hindu and other groups to settle lawsuits filed against the chain for mislabeling French fries and hash browns as vegetarian when the vegetable oil used in their preparation, in fact, contained beef tallow. In addition to putting together a Dietary Practice/Vegetarian Advisory Panel to prevent future problems, McDonald's posted this apology in June of that year:

> We regret we did not provide these customers with complete information, and we sincerely apologize for any hardship that these miscommunications have caused among Hindus, vegetarians and others. . . . We should have done a better job in these areas, and we're committed to doing a better job in the future.

Those were comparably simpler days. Now the challenge will be to convince those with religious and moral prohibitions against eating animals that the injection of pig DNA into a tomato no more makes a tomato porcine than a vaccine turns people into diseases, to see if the vegetarianism of Jainism, Hinduism, and Buddhism, a byproduct of the tenet of nonviolence, which extends to animal life, applies to cultured beef grown in an animal-free serum substitute. Should cultured pork follow beef, will Orthodox Jews be able to skip over Leviticus's

> And the pig, because it has a cloven hoof that is completely split, but will not regurgitate its cud; it is unclean for you. You shall not eat of their flesh, and you shall not touch their carcasses; they are unclean for you

exhortation against the consumption of pork? There is, after all, no carcass. An exemption to the prohibition would seem even more clear-cut to Muslims, as the Quran says, "He has made it unlawful for you, that which dies of itself, the blood and the flesh of the swine and that on which the name of any other than God has been invoked." The pork being consumed is not dead pig, so it should be permissible, but will the faithful see it that way? Will we really be able to call a substance which never lost its breath and never had breath to lose, "meat"? Could man create a "meat" that is somehow neither fake nor real?

* * *

If all plants and animals that had ever been genetically modified were unmitigated successes—no allergic reactions, no agricultural or environmental problems, no deterioration in taste, no religious prohibitions tested—would consumers equate genetically engineered foods and those who make them with something sinister, something fake? Do we see that which can cause harm and that which is fake as fungible in our minds? Why are the borders between junk, *ersatz*, substitute, analogue, engineered, mislabeled, and adulterated foods and that plastic fruit my sister so defiantly ingested porous in both our language and our minds? The artisanal marshmallows made at the local café for your hot (fair trade) chocolate, the Kraft Jet-Puffed marshmallows, and the desiccated marshmallows in your child's box of Lucky Charms are all called marshmallows, but are they all fundamentally the same? Why are they all called marshmallows if they are not made from the same ingredients, or made the same way? Consumers don't seem to care about that, about the impoverishment of names.

A healthy diet is varied; this is true for the earth, too. If you plant the same crops on the same plot of soil over and over again every year without a break, you will destroy that land. When our language is impoverished, we leach words of their meaning as successfully as we do dirt of its nutrients. Humans, for better or worse, have left no inch of this earth untouched. There is no food with which we have not interfered before it reaches our hands and mouths. We have new food but not new thoughts about this food, about the nature of its "reality."

Dr. Frankenstein did not make a monster—the peasants who did not understand Frankenstein's creation were responsible for that development. Food bearing science's heavy handprint must be judged based on its merits, not based on our fears of what we do not understand.

And I do mean must. One of the major effects of climate change in the next decades will be on our diets. We should prepare ourselves for a future where famine is more common and our way of dealing with it may include *ersatz* foods, cultured and analogue proteins, and—well, anything that survives and is edible. Choice will not be in our vocabulary forever.

What we eat is not who we are. Food certainly can shape our bodies and minds, even kill us, but this is not the exclusive ability of food human hands have manipulated. More importantly, "fake" food may not always be healthy or safe, but it cannot make us "fake" people. Only we can do that.

4 WHAT WAS NEVER REAL CAN(NOT) BE FAKED

It's the turn of the twentieth century, and one of the finest minds of his generation has gone missing. He must have seen it coming. Though he did nothing to prevent his abduction, he has left us clues with which to determine the identity and location of his captor. We have forty-five minutes to make our way through the puns, riddles, codes, chess, and string, or our man is doomed. I have never met him, but it's a lot of pressure to have someone else's life in your hands. My heart races, my palms sweat, and I have difficulty concentrating. Halfway through our allotted time we have to pick up the fake antique phone to ask assistance from the fur cape and deerstalker-wearing host watching us like a creep from another room. If this were real life, if the kidnappee were a real man and we, a group of strangers with no detective qualifications, his only hope, the one and only Sherlock Holmes would be dead.

The theme element, and how well or badly it adheres to the time of a fictional or real place in order to tell an interactive story, is what attracted me to escape rooms. What repelled me much more strongly, however, is that a group of people voluntarily pays to be locked in a room from which they have nothing but the word of the host they will ever be released. A couple of times a year, persons in the United States, usually young women, manage to escape from a room where they were unwillingly kept. The women are not playing a game— or they are playing a game, but one in which they did not wish to participate, one in which they did not hand over a credit card and sign a release form with a smile. I have yet to see an escape room experience that emulates or attempts to emulate the trauma of actual kidnap victims. It would be too horrendous, yet we flock to the framework of this most horrendous of crimes. We visit prisons of all kinds—mock, like escape rooms, haunted houses, and mazes, as well as real, like Alcatraz and Robben Island, or an amalgam of both, like Eastern State Penitentiary, a prison-turned-Halloween attraction— and let ourselves be trapped, for a minute or thirty, perversely enjoying the adrenaline rush that comes with well-crafted panic.

Or rather where others do. As much as I love a good puzzle, I find the concept, so explicit in the fiction of the entertainment, the fakeness of the thing already fake, a little too close to non-fiction in its scaffolding. I do not enjoy the rise in heart rate, the sweaty palms, the light-headedness that comes from fear, and I do not really understand why others enjoy places that drape the tapestry of entertainment over one of the worst fates a person can contemplate.

On the other hand, many years ago in the spring of 2004, I had the good fortune to study abroad in London. A former friend from Yale was also in the UK, at Cambridge for a year. One weekend she came down to see me and, along with some other friends, we took the short walk from my flat in Marylebone, a neighborhood optimally nestled between Regent's Park to the north and Hyde Park to the south, to 221B Baker Street, fictional home of Sherlock Holmes and actual, extremely bizarre museum.

Though the Sherlock Holmes Museum also possessed* a study, it could not have been more different from the polished, well-thought-out, panic-inducing escape room I visited in Alexandria, Virginia. Each floor of the Museum depicted either Sherlock's rooms or Sir Arthur Conan Doyle's stories in life-size diorama form, complete with not-particularly-lifelike wax figures of the characters and fake artifacts from the cases. At first, being a child of the modern age, I assumed the figures were Disney-esque animatronics, machine people who might not waggle their eyebrows, but would pretend to smoke a pipe, dash a pen across paper, play the violin, or step backward, aghast at the latest twist in the case.

---

*I use the past tense because I have not visited the museum in many years, and it may be very different now.

Alas, the figures we walked amongst remained frozen and, consequently, incredibly boring. On the top floor we lingered a little longer, tired from the climb through fiction brought to uninspired half-life. In fact, I don't remember a single mannequin in the Sherlock Holmes Museum but one: the bank clerk on the top floor. He was sitting at a desk, and his eyes bugged out of his head, presumably in horror at the snake wrapped around his skull. I remember him for one reason and one reason alone.

That motherfucking snake moved.

I screamed and leapt backward, aghast at the latest twist in the museum. My friends all turned and admonished me for making a ruckus. I pointed to the snake, which was now as static as its prey, and insisted that it wasn't my fault, that the snake had moved. My friends—really, it's a generous term to call people your friends who don't believe you about such important things as sneaky electronic snakes—thought I had gone barmy, which is British for loony tunes. As the seconds passed, and the snake slept, I began to consider they might be right. Nothing else in the museum possessed the power of locomotion. Why would this single snake on the top floor be empowered to strike? Still, I made my unconvinced friends wait and watch. And wait. And watch. And wait just a little—

The snake moved again. "Aha!" I shrieked, vindicated in my sanity, the museum's foray into gaslighting now visible to all. Instead of apologizing, my friends just shrugged their shoulders, and we ventured back downstairs and out of the museum, me still shaking and watching the other figures as we descended for sudden unexpected awakenings.

I still think about that snake, about the evil genius behind that choice. In a very brief moment I was convinced of the snake's reality, and then unsure of my own. Had the wax figures not been so unrealistic, had someone warned me to be on the lookout for one thing that is not like the others, had I known that not all fakes are equal, would I have been for that one instant so surprised and so terrified? Not likely. The snake was small and just as fake-looking as the wax figurines, and no part of the scene conjured up "what if"s for me—I have no worries that I might one day be murdered with a poisonous snake to the head. The power of the display lay, rather, in its improbability, a result of omnipresent counterpoints. The ride got me because I did not know I was on it.

Sherlock-themed escape room and Sherlock Holmes Museum alike are conceits that demand suspension of disbelief that extends beyond its traditional domain. Books and films only require their audiences to believe with their eyes and minds, while these three-dimensional entertainments demand the suspension of the body's disbelief as it moves through a space. It takes less work to make that transition the more ubiquitous the entertainment's subject is in the audience's day-to-day lives. Walking into a theme park, in which you can hug cartoons, take rides through fairy tales, and spend the day in a facsimile of movies based on books, may then be likened to hearing background noise make its way to the forefront. The cultural touchstones visitors see writ large in the park have seeped into their bones long before their visit, which is part of why they visit in the first place. "In the world of simulation, everything doubles back on itself," architecture critic Ada Louise Huxtable says. "The fastest-growing theme park is the re-created movie set or back lot, where the visitor imagines himself an actor in the story on a re-created setting that is a copy of an earlier, unreal place."[1] While as of 2017 Disney World's Pandora and Universal's The Wizarding World of Harry Potter seem to be the most extensive projections into this sort of derivatives of derivatives, nothing beats the Jurassic Park ride based on a movie based on a book about an amusement park. Until someone builds an Austenland theme park, Universal Studios' Jurassic Park ride will win the award for most self-attributive "fake" place.

Ada Louise Huxtable and Jean Baudrillard in the escape room

DISCLOSURE: In order to parse both the widespread emotional disdain for and commercial victory of simulated spaces, I took it upon myself to read two of simulations' greatest critics, the aforementioned Ada Louise Huxtable and Jean Baudrillard, and then promptly get very upset at them. What follows is a borderline rant. Buckle up.

When I was thirteen, my eighth-grade class went on a field trip to Yale University, not far from the town where I grew up, for the express purpose (we all assumed) of cruelly dangling in front of us a collegiate experience so beyond our reach as to be extraterrestrial. Years later, all I remember from my first but not last trip to Yale is something our tour guide told us about the intimidating and impressive architecture of Old Campus, the area of the university reserved for freshmen dorms: it was fake. As renovations took place and new buildings were added, acid was poured down the sides of the walls to age them up so they blended in with the older buildings. New windows were intentionally cracked into "Y" shapes for Yale. My reaction to this information remains the same today as it was then: What a shameful waste of money.

It took a long time for me to shake my disdain for my future alma mater. Simulation within the entertainment structures of the escape room, the Sherlock Holmes Museum, and theme parks shows its seams. Simulation of age under the pretense of a history for the purpose of contextualization, *without disclosure*, looks like fraud. Places as much as food (or people, for that matter) have a responsibility to be honest about what they are, particularly if a financial transaction is taking place. When you purchase tuition, room, and board, you are not just purchasing the professors' time and wisdom, but membership in a culture and history. You want to know that the place you have decided to spend four years and thousands of dollars is being up- front in all things—whether it's the architecture and history of the school, the nature of the meals being served in the dining hall, the credentials of the professors, the crime stats for the surrounding neighborhood, or the actual content of the lessons.

This is not to say contextualism has no place. Though Huxtable, with whom I regret to say we are about to get very acquainted, writes,

> The fallacy of contextualism, the masquerade of matched materials, the cosmetic cover-up of architectural maquillage meant to make a building "fit" surroundings that frequently change, are a trap into which many architects jump or fall through good intentions or self-delusion[2]

the execution and the philosophy of contextualism are not one interchangeable, execrable thing. Much of the past Huxtable idolizes remains in streets and homes and places that have not ridden the wrecking ball into the future, but still remain transformed. Context is inexorable, whether chosen by the architect or the neighborhood or city around it. The Pantheon in Rome is, last time I checked, opposite a McDonald's, which I can guarantee did not exist back in the second century AD; then the Pantheon was a Roman temple, now it's a church, but mostly it's a site for tourists to take Instagram photos. And before the building was completed by Hadrian, an even earlier temple, commissioned by Marcus Agrippa during the reign of Augustus, stood in the same place. Shouldn't we be angry when history knocks history down, when the new obliterates the old, rather than when it makes compromises or attempts to conserve, renovate, or contextualize? Or perhaps we shouldn't be upset about anything and just hope against hope all our demolitions will be ultimately replaced by Pantheons, regardless of how many McDonald's fill their environs.

The Museum of Modern Art (MOMA), the *New York Times*, the *Wall Street Journal*, the Graham Foundation, Carter Wiseman, Robert A. M. Stern, Paul Goldberger, and the Pulitzer Prize committee were all Huxtable fans, but, despite how much I love her name and am impressed she got a book called *Kicked a Building Lately?* published, Ada Louise Huxtable does not seem to offer more than a highly developed aesthetic that she can champion until the other kids hang up their protractors and go home. An egoist of the highest order, Huxtable cannot conceive of an architectural choice that might have merit and yet be unappealing to her, or vice-versa. For all her background, her arguments fall into the *Thinking, Fast and Slow* trap— she is rationalizing her feelings and calling that which doesn't live up to her arbitrary and tenuous standards "unreal" with, no, not even specious arguments but opinions presented as fact. And these opinions are wont to contradict themselves.

People like what they like and try to make reality fit their internal narrative. If Huxtable likes a design, it has "a nostalgic modernism"[3] or "an equally inventive and nostalgic modernism."[4] If she does not, she cries out that "for those without memory, nostalgia fills the void. For those without reference points, novelties are enough. For those without the standards supplied by familiarity with the source, knock-offs will do."[5] Simulation within the confines of modernism is charming; simulation outside, a classist affront.

Huxtable accuses the present generation of self-indulgence, then talks about the modernists of the day she loves.

> When the successes of the theme park and the expediencies of the pop landscape are raised to cult status, when their example is offered by tastemakers as a model for buildings whose role and image are intrinsic to a different and more traditional set of needs and values, or are used to bypass tough solutions to nontraditional problems, something very peculiar occurs. You get faux populism as high art. I think the word "faux," or "fake," fits; it is everywhere today, because it is so right for what is so wrong. Skewed in meaning, rather than indicating falseness, it gives a stamp of approval to the blatantly unreal, a suggestion of class to the frankly inferior. Using the French faux makes the fake chic; it gives the phony cachet. It goes with the same state of mind that sees architecture as gift wrap and accepts tarted-up history. Something real has been perverted, and something important has been abdicated. The result is faux architecture.[6]

Such non-specific phrasings as "something real" and "something important" do not constitute good lawyering, nor do pointing out all the things you dislike and going "ew, barf" win over many a jury.

While her disdain for an under-defined "faux" is problematic, Huxtable is not without some salient points on the potential problems of simulation in and outside architecture, particularly regarding imitations of imitations, like the clone of a clone that occurs in *The Prestige*. Where she sees a diminishment of imagination, invention, and good taste, science sees something called "generation loss," in which copies of copies, moving on down, are in ever-increasing danger of losing integrity. While this is one way of looking at what has occurred to the modern landscape of America, what was sharp becoming blurry, what was extraordinary losing faith with a sort of molecular pixelation,* the metaphor could just as easily be inverted, as in the case of Russian nesting dolls. The difference between the largest Russian doll and the smallest is not simply in size or in their details, but their experience of the world and our experience of them. For us, the largest doll appears to be the original, with every subsequent internal doll a smaller, less detailed iteration. But the smallest doll is solid and constructed differently from the dolls that have subsumed her. It is the larger ones that, we realize eventually, must

---

*Not to be confused with pixilation, which is either a stop-motion technique where live actors are made to look animated or the state of being mentally unbalanced.

come after. They have expanded upon the kernel of the idea that is the heart doll, and while she may disappear inside them, she remains at their core. In some ways they make her more special: Look what has been created in her image, a many-layered hive of homage.

The simulation-bashing Statler to Ada Louise Huxtable's Waldorf was postmodern French philosopher and unsupportable ass Jean Baudrillard, who didn't just have a problem with amusement parks and their complicated fakeness, but museums as well—and I do not mean "museums" like the Sherlock Holmes Museum.

Consider the Lascaux caves of Baudrillard's home country. Parietal art, commonly referred to as cave wall paintings, is as—or more—important for what it tells us about the evolution of mankind than it is for the aesthetics of the imagery itself. For investigators to do their work and for the paintings to be preserved, the general public must not be allowed to enter the caves and still expect the caves and their paintings to remain in the same conditions as when they were discovered. But Baudrillard was under the impression that museums have a nefarious purpose for providing simulations: to strip real things of their singularity, turn them obsolete, hide them away from the cheated masses, for the sake of profit and, presumably, as an opportunity for the board to practice their maniacal cackling.

With the pretext of saving the original, one forbade visitors to enter the Lascaux caves, but an exact replica was constructed five hundred meters from it, so that everyone could see them (one glances through a peephole at the authentic cave, and then one visits the reconstituted whole).[7]

Baudrillard continues, "from now on there is no longer a difference: the duplication suffices to render both artificial." Mwahaha, surely.

Museums and their ilk do their best to steal time and arrest deterioration, but this is not the nature of a universe studded with humans. To acknowledge the limits of conservation by creating replicas of artifacts and fossils is not to make all exhibits artificial but to embrace the iteration of objects and to satisfy the public curiosity of the Now while fulfilling our responsibility to future generations by giving them an opportunity to experience Lascaux as well. When authorities are not thoughtful about conserving historical finds, what occurs is vandalism, theft, ruin of ruins. Conservation is about acknowledging a reality that has not changed throughout human history—men have grubby hearts and even grubbier fingers.

Immediately south of Dulles Airport in Northern Virginia in a large hangar all its own resides the Steven F. Udvar-Hazy Center, the annex to the Smithsonian's Air and Space Museum. Inside stand and hang all manner of space- and aircraft, from planes and jets to helicopters and gliders, as well as missiles, suits, and related accoutrements, representing the sum history of mechanized flight, manned and otherwise. While models abound, much of the aircraft is artifact. The Lockheed SR-72 Blackbird, the world's fastest jet-propelled aircraft, is the real deal. In the spring of 1990 it took off from Los Angeles, and an hour, four minutes, and twenty seconds later set down at Dulles, at which point it was turned over to the Smithsonian. The Concorde is real. The Space Shuttle *Discovery*, with all its silica tiles, spent a total of 365 days in space and flew 133 missions.

But in some places history is modified for preservation purposes. For example, the Apollo 11 flotation collar, the actual unit deployed during the recovery of Apollo 11, is kept separate from its Command Module *Columbia*. To get the full sense of the collar's purpose and still preserve the more fragile Command Module, it is displayed with an "egress trainer," a simulator module used by the astronauts to practice exiting the Command Module post-splashdown. According to Allan Needell, Curator of Space History at the National Air and Space Museum,

When we decided to restore and display the Apollo 11 flotation collar, the Command Module *Columbia* was already on display on a special mount and under a Plexiglas cover in the Museum's central Milestones Gallery. Altering that display was not an option. Because the egress trainer had made use of flotation collars we thought the next best place to display it was on an artifact that actually had once had one attached. Future display of *Columbia* will be in specially constructed cases that are currently being designed and fabricated. For various display and conservation reasons it has been determined that it can be best observed without the collar.[8]

In tune with Baudrillard's insistence that simulation sucks the souls from places like Azkabanian Dementors, Huxtable believes that artifacts have the same vulnerability, writing, "the copy [of an ancient Egyptian statue] corrupts the original because it has eliminated the sensibility triggered in part by the miracle of survival and the messages the object brings from the past—just those things that generate the response to the work of art."[9] But how? By incorporating the egress trainer into the display, the collar is able to show its function and proper form. Without it, the collar would just be easily passed by, context-free paraphernalia. A placard accompanying the collar clarifies that the command module presented is not Command Module *Columbia*, and I believe it is fair to assert that neither the Command Module nor the egress trainer are rendered fake for the choice. An Egyptian statue too fragile for public viewing can be lost forever, or a double can be produced, properly labeled, and provide identical information and, yes, even awe. I can't tell if Baudrillard and Huxtable are presuming extreme sensitivity to the aura of history radiating from artifacts or some kind of middle-class brain lesion that prevents visitors to Lascaux from observing the replica of the paintings and experiencing a sense of wonder at such a remarkable discovery, despite the single degree of remove. Why on Earth should we see a copy of an ancient Egyptian statue, cave wall replica, or model for a space shuttle and lose our sense of history or art, our ability to discern between the genuine article and that which isn't, or our ability to marvel at what man hath wrought and continues to work*?

Sometimes humanity regrets taking the course of compromise, and perhaps it's greedy to want to both preserve history and experience it at the same time, but we are a remarkable species capable of both great good and great evil. Where no malicious intent is present and where no cancers result, I say we celebrate. Our desperate attempts to capture butterflies never work the way we want them to; we can only pin their wings and not their flight. Let us then take what we can get from museums and be grateful.

Because, to really bring the point home, the big difference between this conversation and the one on "fake food" is that all manmade or man-touched objects and places are unnatural, unreal. Lascaux is remarkable in that some of our Upper Paleolithic ancestors looked at those blank cave walls and said, "Ugh, boring. Let's draw some pictures of this morning's hunt on there and jazz it up a bit." We have ancient Egyptian statues to "simulate" in the first place because, again, ancient Egyptians looked at trees and said, "I don't get it. What if I used my knife and cut the tree so it looked like

---

*It's true. "Wrought" is the past tense of "work." Massively disappointing, huh?

our king instead? Maybe we can get a deal on our taxes." We have both the Command Module *Columbia* and its egress trainer because, though we have minds that can breach an atmosphere that our bodies naturally cannot, we need to simulate that act before we do it in real life to get it right. In their service to the public's education and edification, copies and models are real parts of the story of the invented objects and places with which they share form.

People are bound to make mistakes, what with not having time travel and mind reading and all. So if time travel is no more possible than building a bubble complete with vacuum around the past, three options remain: recreating with an eye to authenticity, acknowledging that being human means being fallible and likely to mess it up; recreating without paying any mind to the details and just going for the spirit; or letting the past stay in the past where it belongs. All of these responses have merit, and none of them are satisfactory for Huxtable, or for any of us. They require either time to work differently, or people to.

The real, desirable things are delicate, and humans are vehicles of destruction. The oil on our fingertips, the clumsiness of our grip, our breath, our sweat, our diseases—we are the Grim Reapers for our own artistic achievements. We make delicate masterpieces, and then we cordon them off, dim the lights, and say "No touching!" The flag known as the Star-Spangled Banner is kept behind glass in the Smithsonian's National Museum of American History. Since 1998, when it was taken out of the Hall of Flags and deemed too frail to hang ever again, it has lain flat in a darkened room where no cameras are allowed, because the flag is important, sacred, must not be harmed. What's funny is the flag is already tarnished and torn, snippings of it cut out by its erstwhile owners who wanted to offer, Ariel Sabar says, "citizens of a rising nation a tether to their past. A similar instinct survives today, in the almost talismanic power that attaches to chunks of the Berlin Wall or steel from the ruins of the World Trade Center."[10] And, in fact, just across the street from the American History Museum, at the Ronald Reagan Building and International Trade Center, a segment of the Berlin Wall stands next to the exit. A sign beside it, however, reads, "Please do not touch." Today's tethers are hands-off.

Present-day Americans would never call mass-reproduced flags "fake," and they would never disrespect one by cutting squares from one to serve as souvenirs. And yet why not, when this is the history of the original? We cannot simultaneously interact and preserve, but why would we want to preserve something with which we can't have interaction? We are a species fond of paradox.

One must recognize, first, the limits of organic material—paper, bones, fabrics, wood, etc.—that make up the vast majority of cultural artifacts and the things we most want to preserve, the things that matter most to us, and, second, access to originals is not merely restricted by the cost and distance of museums, but the restrictions required for preservation purposes, which keep us at arm's length, in shadow, and temporally removed from the art.

Though cracks and chips in art, artifacts, and architecture, as indicators of a life thoroughly lived, are more authentic, down that path annihilation lounges in a tree and files its claws by the light of a full moon. Huxtable's belief that there is no substitute for primary and repeated sensory exposure to a work of art for connoisseurship may be true, but it is impractical, particularly when it comes to the "tactile sensation,"[11] since any handling of work demands gloves and delicacy. Huxtable is claiming a poverty of artistic experience for those without exceptional access, but it is her interaction with art that must be impoverished if it falters when confronted by the essentially gossamer barriers between the public and objects worth our admiration and preservation.

Which, then, am I suggesting: that the Guggenheim allow visitors to take a pair of scissors to its Jackson Pollocks (though what would be the difference?), or that it hide its Pollocks in a vault and only display fakes the public can touch and destroy to their heart's content? Neither. I am saying art is not just a visual experience for the painter; it's a physical experience. We treat art as cake too pretty to eat, but a painter does not make a painting to put in a museum to be seen for only a minute before the guest moves on to the next picture. She wants a large audience and a long audience, an audience that will be moved and continue to be moved by her work long after their day is over. Twisted up in these discussions of art and architecture—be they museums and the works they display or archives, ruins, restored historic locations, or buildings that have withstood the test of time without falling apart or requiring upkeep—is the idea of common memory, that our historical memory is as vulnerable to erosion and degradation as bricks, if not more so. While Baudrillard and Huxtable may think simulations and copies steal authenticity, value, and identity from the object or place witnessed, that idea discounts the whole psychology of souvenirs. Our reason for indulging in souvenirs in the first place is right there in the name—*souvenir*, French for memory. We are buying memories, personal experience in a plastic detail. We only have so much space in our deteriorating brains. If we buy a magnet with Van Gogh's *Irises* on them, every time we go to the refrigerator we can remember that vacation when we visited the Getty in Los Angeles—driving south on Sepulveda from the Valley with a parent, sibling, or romantic partner, learning about a new song from the high school students there on a field trip, wondering at the majesty of this famous painting, afterward going to dinner on Beverly and a show at Largo at the Coronet, or heading west to Santa Monica and a movie at the Aero, the freak rainstorm and rainbow afterward—these moments that we infuse into the magnet upon purchase and when we see it. And if specific events are lost, the feelings may remain. Fragments of the past are tracked in with the present, and so money is converted into a token of identity. If the painting is turned into a purchasable print to be brought home, the sculpture turned small and plastic and attached to a keychain, it becomes a part of our days and lives, and still allows the original to survive in dim light, behind a black tape line, and/or under the watchful gaze of a security guard.

There is no perfect substitute for an original, but the alternatives we provide when the original is unavailable for viewing or physical contact or purchase to bring home don't take anything away from the original, but rather add to it the breadth of its influence on the culture and the individuals with which it comes into contact, second-degree or otherwise.

*　　*　　*

In the future, the equation of "fake places" to architecture that doesn't respect its elders may become a quaint notion. As oceans rise, deserts expand, and weather becomes more extreme, mankind will have two choices: take nature's punishment for all the greenhouse gas (GHG) we emitted, or continue to use artificial means to create livable environments. I say "continue" because humans have been taking land back since the invention of dams and levees and the reclamation of earth where before there was none—from the Netherlands and Venice to the Palm Islands of Dubai. The number of coastal cities and low-lying areas, including Houston, New York, New Orleans, much of Florida, Bangladesh, and London, which will need extraordinary measures to survive into the next century, are countless. Where will their residents go if the price to remain is too high? Hundreds of millions of people may be required to move in only a few decades, a number that would constitute the largest mass migration in history—greater than the settling of the Americas and the slave trade, greater than the displacement caused by both World Wars combined, greater than any event in any time in human civilization. And where, I ask again, will they go?

Huxtable claims that casino guests who have been to the Amazon on package tours prefer simulated rain forests like the indoor one at Las Vegas's Mirage Resort & Casino to the actual South American jungle. The Mirage's simulation, obviously, has a lot going for it: snakes and jaguars don't hide in the trees, there are no mosquitoes sinking malaria or yellow fever into visitors' broken skin, and it's not just closer than Brazil—it's also compact by design.[*]

What if this simulated rainforest, by diverting polluting tourists, helped increase the life expectancy of the actual rainforest? Would that make it good? What if this were the only rainforest left that humans could still visit, since all other rainforests will, in all likelihood, soon become too hot for people to survive in? Would that make it real?

The planet has been so plasticized, overburdened, and razed that it makes sense those responsible for its damage wish to preserve and rewrite history all at the same time. We are up against a literal and figurative desertification of our planet, resources and habitable space decreasing as thirst for something unspoiled by our poisonous manipulations

---

[*]As opposed to size reduction by slash-and-burn.

increases. Beyond mankind's sand castles, "real" mirages wink in and out of our vision. We hate them for how pretty and ephemeral they are, and so we build virtual reality worlds to keep them from vanishing with the heat.

Simulation in that sense can act as a soothing but enervating balm in a time when the survival of our species cannot afford it. "But ultimately, it is not the way something looks, or how that look is achieved, that is of primary importance," as Huxtable writes. "What matters is what it does."[12] I agree, but even more essential than whether places fulfill the promises they make to us is whether we, as residents and visitors rather than architects or curators, meet our obligations to places. The only true frauds and fakes aren't the art and architecture we create and recreate, but ourselves when we sell places as being more or less than what they are or are delinquent as caretakers of both our cultural and environmental heritage. Ultimately, loss of integrity is not the result of alteration, restoration, or imitation of the objects and places—of "simulation"—but of disingenuousness among men.

5 HIPPOPOTAMUS TEETH

George Washington had hippopotamus teeth. Not wooden teeth. Teeth made of hippopotamus ivory.

George Washington had elephant teeth. Not wooden teeth. Teeth made of elephant ivory.

George Washington had slave teeth. Not wooden teeth. Teeth taken from the mouths of slaves.

Just as humans have been turning themselves into cyborgs in stories since long before the advent of science fiction—mythology just called them different names: centaur (half horse), satyr (half goat), harpy (half bird), mermaid (half fish), sphinx (half lion), minotaur (half bull)—humans were, in reality, turning themselves into cyborgs long before computers, even prior to the industrial revolution. Though I have found no name for those ancient humans who employed prosthetics, archaeologists have dug up ample evidence that humans have indeed been filling the lacunae provided by bad medicine and worse luck for millennia: the earliest known prosthesis is a 3,000-year-old wooden toe found on an

Egyptian mummy. But let's start with someone a little closer to home whose name is apocryphally synonymous with one of the smaller artificial body parts: George Washington.

Teeth made of wood wouldn't have made a lick of sense.* Washington's saliva would have rotten the teeth right out of his mouth, and his tongue would have been riddled with cuts and slivers. Worse, the General and then President would have looked absurd, because wood does not resemble bone and enamel. And the key to a proper fake, to a substitution that does what it was meant to do, is that it not just be able to do the job of the teacher that's out sick, but that it intimate a teacher: a substitute teacher that doesn't look like a teacher doesn't survive the school day. A substitute prosthetic that doesn't look the corresponding body part doesn't survive the free market.

In the 1770s, presumably as grossed out as we would be at the idea of dead people or animal teeth in our mouths, a pharmacist with the impossibly French name of Alexis Duchateau made the first set of porcelain dentures. They weren't sufficiently proximate to the real deal, however, and, in the UK at least, something called "Waterloo teeth" remained far more popular.

Waterloo teeth. Everyone has watched enough Second World War movies to know that few soldiers had qualms about relieving their deceased enemies (and sometimes

---

*Don't front. You love the pun as much as I do.

friends) of boots, jackets, watches, and other possessions the moldering could no longer use. In previous centuries this looting extended to dead soldiers' teeth. Rachel Bairsto of the British Dental Association wrote that she found no evidence the public knew the pulp, dentin, and enamel they were putting in their mouths were the original property of their sons or the men who had killed their sons.[1] But they knew they were coming from somewhere—the living poor or the grave-robbed dead—and made their choices with a knowledge, however subconscious, that many of us couldn't imagine bearing in the twenty-first century.

Thankfully dentistry progressed, requiring training and certification, and we no longer have to make those decisions. Modern dental prosthetics, typically fashioned from acrylic resin or a more agreeable porcelain than Duchateau's, do the job of one's old teeth and, more importantly to many, look just like them as well. However, complex feelings over not just the other defects and derelictions of our flesh and bone, but the objects that rectify our death-obsessed bodies, remain.

When it comes to imitation of human anatomy, fakes, be they artificial eyes, dentures, breast implants, prosthetic limbs, or mechanical heart valves, exist for one reason and one reason alone: our bodies tend to fail incrementally. Hair falls out in the shower, teeth are shoved out by more teeth or by decay, eyes and limbs are subject to trauma, organs deteriorate, and breasts threaten.

Westerners don't think of some of these things as qualitatively the same. A patient with valvular heart disease needs the pyrolitic carbon or bioprosthetic replacement to survive, while no one has ever died *directly* from lack of breast implants, but that doesn't mean both aren't deemed "necessary." Need is situational, and the human body, an unsustainable machine run by an operating system with no more complex a primary directive than "GO ON," is not above self-deception. There is a blurry line between cosmetic alterations, perceived as being undertaken to fake youth out of a fear of death or irrelevance (collagen injections, hair dye, follicle implants—is baldness in men comparable to a flat chest in women?), and the transplants and prosthetics people employ to actually keep degradation off their backs and insure that their lives are fully lived. And there is shame in any of these procedures and aftercare, regardless of the form of need. We treat our bodies and their trials not as naturally weak shells, but as mirrors of what we have done, what we deserve, and what we think God or the universe believes we deserve. A woman who runs every day, a woman who eats nothing but salads and lentil soups, may get breast cancer and lose what makes her whole. A woman, with all the eyes of the world on her, may still not feel herself enough, or "complete." Breasts are not given out evenly or proportionately, and how we are perceived by others and how it changes what they give us because of how we look—respect, opportunity, love, work opportunities—is vital. A man may smoke every day of his life, and his body may not be able to handle it. A boy may be born with a congenital heart defect, and his father may blame himself, his smoking in the same room as his wife. The mother may blame herself. It doesn't matter what the doctors say—no one is broken without shame or guilt. Society doesn't allow people to go through surgeries of this sort without being considered weak, or broken, or lesser in some way. They may have survived, they may be better, 2.0 versions of the selves that went under the knife, but it is difficult to forget that in one way or another their bodies temporarily betrayed them and will one day betray them again, permanently, and so us. No matter how much plastic or metal we put in ourselves, none of us will win.

Still, Fitzgerald-like, man continues to beat back against the current of his mortality, encouraged by ever-improving innovation, starting with an inventor from Birmingham, England, named Alexander Parkes, who patented the first thermoplastic, nitrocellulose, in 1856. Usable as a low-grade explosive, guncotton, as Parkes's invention was called, soon found its way into warheads, naval mines, and torpedoes, all in time for the advent of the American Civil War.

"In combination with rifled, breech-loading artillery pieces, high-explosive shells could wreak much greater damage than the solid balls of earlier cannon,"[2] that greater damage including higher death and amputation rates. It is no surprise then that it was in the 1860s (1862 to be precise) that the US Congress first started appropriating money to purchase artificial limbs for military personnel. By 1866, the War Department, now the Department of Defense, was replacing those limbs every five years thanks to Parkes, truly the Alfred Nobel of his time. In 1921 the responsibility of caring for veterans' prosthetics transferred to the Veterans Bureau, now the Department of Veterans Affairs, and has remained there ever since.

In Edgar Allan Poe's pre–Civil War short story, "The Man That Was Used Up," the narrator meets in passing Brevet Brigadier General John A. B. C. Smith, a man who seems to be not merely a man but the consummate embodiment of a man. "There was an *air distingue* pervading the whole man, which spoke of high breeding, and hinted at high birth," the narrator says of Smith, a war hero whose perfect looks imply, to the narrator, internal perfections—a common logical misstep, like, say, believing that a rich person would be better at being Secretary of Commerce than a poor person. When our narrator says Smith's shoulders "would have called up a blush of conscious inferiority into the countenance of the marble Apollo,"[3] the author foreshadows the reveal that Smith is more than man—perhaps art, perhaps god.

Compounding "the odd air of je ne sais quoi which hung about [his] new acquaintance" is the fact that everyone the narrator encounters seems to know a secret about the General. Alas, these individuals in the know are stingy with their gossip and are without exception cut off at some variation on the line, "Why, bless me, he's the man—"

Finally, the narrator, overcome by curiosity as to what follows these titillating em-dashes, goes to visit the source. Barging into Smith's bedroom despite being told that its occupant is in the middle of dressing, the narrator discovers the General quite literally undone, his body in disassembled parts.

Disregarding the fact that the narrator is unfathomably rude, imagine forcing yourself unannounced into the bedroom of a war hero with no expectation of being killed for the audacity. I hate to say it, but the 1830s appear to have been a more trusting time.

Anyway, Smith has indeed earned his reputation, but rather than wear his "scratches" with pride (he would be but a one-legged, one-armed torso with no jaw, the story suggests), Smith has purchased his remarkable body from a variety of purveyors. Those superior shoulders our narrator admired are, in fact, not nature's work, but the work of some gentleman named Pettit (apparently the French have put one over on the Italians and their Pythian Apollo). All the other physicals aspects of Smith, which put together constitute such a fine figure, were similarly acquired from this manufacturer or the other. Though it seems highly likely that the extent of Smith's damage is well-known, Smith has neither fear nor shame, for he is still, when collected, an ideal specimen and clearly enjoys the respect and admiration of society. The violence perpetrated upon him by those "dreadful creatures, those Indians" has not disfigured Smith publically, and so the horror with which the public perceives their hero is one coupled with fascination and delight. Having seen Smith in private, in pieces, however, the narrator's opinion is, at least temporarily, tainted—Smith, the product of this "wonderfully inventive age" everyone is espousing, is still to the narrator "the man—the man that was used up."

Nothing is more human than vulnerability, but when confronted with the view of the General, who is missing so much of himself, donning his prosthetics, Poe's narrator deems the General "used up." War used him up and spat him back out, and yet he is still around, a living reminder of what we "should" look like, but also what we can.

A nature without flaws is not of nature, and Poe's narrator subconsciously knows that. To be human has always been, like it or not, to be mortal—man must needs break, wear down, decompose, die. If industrialization has indeed allowed us to surpass nature, then isn't our attachment to our original form obsolete? If we decide that, since the artificial means of patching up our bodies and extending our lives is the product of human intelligence, it must be considered a part of evolution as authentic and natural as anything genetic, then we must let go our idea of what a "real" human looks and sounds like. If the product of our real minds is absorbed into and utilized by the body, how can that product be referred to as artifice? And what does it matter then if the product is flesh-imitating silicone or unembarrassed steel? In Poe's story, the narrator initially positively compares Smith to a masterpiece, better than man. First art, and now technology, has decided the blueprint for the ideal human form, and we have allowed it while condemning it, paradoxically acknowledging that to strive toward perfection is noble, but achieving it is blasphemy, an affront against

God, Nature, and, most importantly, each other. This is why implants, airbrushing, and other such "lies" and "fakes" are so reviled—they serve as reminders of our mortality, that others are engaging in tricks to appear unmarred by the traumas of life. It reminds us we are imperfect, unimproved, fragile in our realness. The narrator in Poe's story is not jealous of the General when he thinks him oddly stunning in stature, just curious. Then, having seen the General vulnerable in his jigsaw state, the narrator is put out. He is seeing death skirted.

"Before I had the prosthesis, I was just a one-sided person,"[4] says Artie McAuley, a veteran who lost his full arm and went without a prosthetic for several decades until volunteering to try out the prototype for the Luke Arm,* echoing the language of Poe's story.

In the documentary *Out on a Limb*, one amputee says, "Up to the Iraqi War, [non-military amputees] were closet people." Another amputee adds, "So there was a lot of shame. And there was a whole shift of consciousness when legs went from being passive ball-and-chains to highly functional. So when that happens, you don't mind saying, 'Yeah, that's my artificial leg.'"

Of course "the better an artificial limb, the fewer limits on a person's independence,"[5] but it is interesting that, for

---

*Developed by DARPA's Revolutionizing Prosthetics and manufactured by Mobius Bionics. Named after Luke Skywalker, who employs a bionic prosthetic hand in *Return of the Jedi*.

at least this particular amputee, shame or pride stemming from the quality of the prosthetic—how much it resembles in form and function an actual limb—seems to outweigh any embarrassment related to the reason its owner has the prosthetic or the vulnerability of flesh it represents. The quality of the fake matters, so, though the vast majority of amputees aren't veterans at all, the military is both one reason why non-veterans may experience comparative shame about limb loss and one reason why they may be proud of the caliber of their prosthetics.

According to the Amputee Coalition, approximately two million people in the United States are living with limb loss, only 45 percent of them from trauma, another 54 percent stemming from vascular diseases including diabetes and peripheral arterial disease, and less than 2 percent from cancer. With an estimated 185,000 amputations a year in the United States, one should note that between 2001 and 2015 major limb amputations from Operation Iraqi Freedom through Freedom's Sentinel only accounted for 1,645 of these amputations total. Yet when we think of amputees, we still think of soldiers, over 150 years after the end of the Civil War.[6]

The overrepresentation of soldiers in our media and thoughts when it comes to prosthetics is in part thanks to and the reason for the advancements out of the US Department of Defense's robotics-and-stuff lab, DARPA (or Defense Advanced Research Projects Agency, for those of you less acronymically inclined)—the people behind the Luke Arm and other prosthetic innovations.

Launched by the Department of Defense as the Advanced Research Projects Agency in 1958, the main purpose of ARPA, as it was then called, was to nerd-kick Sputnik I's ass. Over the last several decades DARPA (the name as of March 1972) has succeeded in putting the Commies in their inferior military-industrial-complex place by not only developing better ways of murdering people through such inventions as ballistic missile defense, but also ways of improving the lives of survivors, such as through their Revolutionizing Prosthetics program. You have to love the American military—even the name of their prosthetics program makes you want to pump your fist. More than simply following through on a responsibility to the men and women of the armed forces who put their lives on the line and sacrificed parts of their bodies to protect our country, DARPA's chief aim is "to continue increasing functionality of the DARPA arm systems so servicemembers with arm loss may one day have the option of choosing to return to duty."[7] The duty of the military is to the military, and any side benefits—of which we must admit there are many—autonomous navigation, the friggin' Internet—are just our luck. "Additionally," the Revolutionary Prosthetics site adds, "the dexterous hand capabilities developed under the program have already been applied to small robotic systems used in manipulating unexploded ordnance, therefore keeping soldiers out of situations that have led to limb loss." In other words, don't look the gift robot in the mouth because you don't know where it's putting that unexploded ordnance once it's done with it.

Lived reality and Edward Scissorhands

For veterans, bodily absences are souvenirs of violence, while outside of war the vacation of limbs is most often a story of disease or trauma that might have been avoided or not, an act of stupidity or of God. Prostheses under any circumstance serve as second chances, but also as reminders of these traumas. It is no wonder that anxiety, social isolation, decreased sexual activity, and depression are common amongst amputees and that "amputation-related body image concerns and perceived social stigma are significant and independent predictors of depression."[8] How we see ourselves and others is how we believe others see us.

Some people could have all their flesh and blood replaced with inorganic materials and always feel "real" and "human," while others have never had so much as a hair dyed and feel like "monsters" or "fakes." Most often transplant patients and those with prosthetics take no notice of their organ or prosthetic until it is not doing its job, causing them pain, or failing them in some other unspecified way—or is brought to their attention through social interaction.

Baudrillard would be a terrible person for anyone with a prosthetic to encounter. His statements about man's vulnerability to machine, that "when the prosthesis goes deeper, is interiorized in, infiltrates the anonymous and micro-molecular heart of the body, as soon as it is imposed on the body itself as the 'original' model, burning all the previous symbolic circuits, the only possible body the immutable repetition of the prosthesis, then it is the end of the body, of its history, and of its vicissitudes"[9] suggests he envisions a technology with the capacity to corrupt the human soul in the way that computer viruses can corrupt computers, or in the way that actual viruses can corrupt actual human organs. While it is not impossible that, in the showdown between flesh and technology, technology may both literally and figuratively make such inroads into human bodies and minds that *Homo sapiens sapiens* is no longer recognizable and is archived in the halls of natural history museums alongside *Homo neanderthalensis*, the theory of prosthesis as a tool for humanity's self-destruction has an inherent fatal flaw. Prosthesis is already humanoid. The prosthesis's entire reason for being is to service the body, to be subsumed and utilized by it, to be as leg or arm. As long as this remains true of our prosthetics, artificial enhancements and substitutes—and there is no indication that this in danger of changing—man retains his humanity, humanizing and de-machinating the machine parts of him, and Baudrillard's "point of no return" is kept at bay. It is only if and when in the course of innovation mechanical man so betters the original, the "natural," that he makes his predecessor obsolete and, as is his duty as a progress-obsessed species, obliterates him, that the machine might become the life force and insert itself between humanity as we know it and its retirement. Should we finally best ourselves, we may not call the upgrade from *Homo sapiens*

sapiens species suicide (though it will be of a sort), but we will be what we have fashioned ourselves into.

In the classic Tim Burton film *Edward Scissorhands*, our hero does not use his scissor hands to take over the world he is forced into, any more than he chooses any aspect of his life in the first place; faulty creation and all subsequent events are decided for him by others. An elderly Kim (Winona Ryder), Edward's once-upon-a-time love interest, begins the tale with

A long time ago, an inventor lived in that mansion. He made many things, I suppose. He also created a man. He gave him insides, a heart, a brain . . . everything. Well, almost everything. You see, the inventor was very old. He died before he got to finish the man he invented. So the man was left by himself, incomplete and all alone.

There is no subtext. Physically incomplete and physically alone is tantamount to emotionally incomplete and emotionally alone.

When Peg Boggs, an Avon lady who is having a bad sales day, makes her way up to the local creepy dark mansion on the hill and meets Edward with his blade-mad hands, Peg asks him, "What happened to you?" An entirely self-aware Edward replies, "I'm not finished." Edward is not blind to who he is. From the media, and the education he received from his father/inventor, Edward is attuned to what the socialized world's ideal looks like, as well as the unlikelihood of him rising to that ideal. However, the viewer sees among

Edward's few possessions a newspaper clipping with the headline, "Boy born without eyes reads with his hands." Disabilities, like the scissor hands, may not be optimal, but they can be overcome.

This is how Edward is treated throughout the movie, not as an artificial man, or a man with a prosthetic, but as a man with a unique disability capable of both great invention and destruction.

The town falls in love with Edward. He becomes so famous for his work cutting topiary, dog hair, and human hair that he ends up on a local TV show. A woman in the audience asks, "Have you ever thought of having corrective surgery or prosthetics? I know a doctor that might be able to help you." Though the scissors are what makes Edward stand out in the community and being different is why he is adored—a respite from the mundane everyday—he says he would like to meet the doctor. The next woman in the audience says, "But if you had regular hands, you'd be like everyone else." Another woman: "But then no one would think you were special. You wouldn't be on TV or anything." To which Peg responds, "No matter what, Edward will always be special."

You remember the rest of the movie—Edward gets roped into burglarizing a neighborhood house, the community turns against him just as Peg's daughter Kim falls in love with him, and Edward is forced to flee those who first objectified him and then decided he was disposable. In the end, Edward is left alone in the mansion on the hill with nothing but his topiary and ice sculptures (who is shipping him big blocks of ice is a question that never gets answered) for company. Though the lesson is that the neighborhood isn't good enough for him, isn't human enough, the result is still the same—banishment.

If the real problem were the hands, then the solution that is presented in the movie—a more pragmatic prosthesis—would be the answer. But the problem is never Edward, but a combination of objectification and a lack of trust on the part of those around him. From the very beginning, Edward is seen less as a person and more as a plaything or distraction for the bored and boring neighborhood. When he turns out to be "real"—someone who makes mistakes—he is cast out. Though his frustration with his hands is always obvious, it's not entirely clear how Edward sees himself, willing as he is to be manipulated like a doll to gain the affection and acceptance of others, until he is abused. Once he sees himself as the object of hate and fear, Edward realizes that the person he knows he is has become imperceptible to others. Justifiably feeling betrayed and hurt, Edward rejects the neighborhood as they reject him.

As fond as I am of *Edward Scissorhands*, the framing fails the spirit of the story. First, this isn't a fairy tale, but a story of deeming others irredeemable too quickly, of making final judgments, of giving up. Second, and most importantly, is that we actually have no idea what Edward thought about any of this. In fact, Edward has very few lines throughout the movie, his voice taken by those who put their own fantasies and fears on him without trying to figure out what he wants, needs, and feels. The only way Edward has of expressing himself is through his scissors, and one imagines that if they were taken away he would be rendered mute. But all of this is uncertain, as the story is told and colored by Kim and her memory, her perception. Edward's point of view is interpreted, yes, by someone who loved him, but also someone who both romanticized him and wasn't willing to go back to him long after he was out of danger from the neighborhood. She is the most untrustworthy of narrators, and yet the most typical. The person who recounts a brief relationship with a "freak" and how it affected his or her life has not changed since Poe's stories.

Unless this was Tim Burton's point: that we will continue to mistake men for monsters as long as we don't let people who don't look like us or have similar backgrounds tell their own stories. In our focus on the future and fantasy, we cannot ignore the lived reality of those who currently possess prosthetics that are as far from making them cyborgs as those ivory teeth were from making George Washington a hippopotamus. This is not only a problem of art but also of academia. Vivian Sobchack, an amputee with a prosthetic left leg, clarifies her experience:

> Although I never really feel as though my prosthetic leg possesses the agency or subjectivity to "turn against" me, I admit that it does have the capacity to become opaque, to turn into a hermeneutic object that I have to pay attention

to and interpret and do something about (other than transparently walk with it). That is, my leg is transformed metonymically at times to another (inhuman) species of thing—the prosthetic resisting its formerly organic function in an ensemble of action directed elsewhere. In these moments, it becomes an absolute other.[10]

While Sobchack goes on to say that she doesn't intend to suggest that autobiographical experience provides a more or less authentic discursive experience, it is also essential to remember that amputees and their prosthetics aren't simply metaphor or fodder for fairy tales and science fiction, but real people with real injuries that medicine and technology are trying to repair. Any conversation about wooden teeth or bionic arms, chimera or cyborgs, needs to be grounded in current reality and not forget the voices of those who undergo the experience of amputation and reconstitution. "Not only do I see myself as fully human (if hardly singular or glamorous)," Sobchack says, "but I also know intimately my prosthetic leg's essential inertia and lack of motivating volition. Indeed, for all the weight that I place on it, it does not run my life."[11]

The future corporeal

In the 1995 animated classic *Ghost in the Shell*, in which whole-body prosthesis is the inevitable result of our technological advancements, Major Motoko Kusanagi insists that it is the mind far more than the facade that constitutes one's humanity and individuality.

"There are countless ingredients that make up the human body and mind, like all the components that make up me as an individual with my own personality. Sure I have a face and voice to distinguish myself from others, but my thoughts and memories are unique only to me, and I carry a sense of my own destiny," Kusanagi says. "Each of those things are just a small part of it. I collect information to use in my own way. All of that blends to create a mixture that forms me and gives rise to my conscience. I feel confined, only free to expand myself within boundaries."

If the plasticization of the human body is inevitable, then the insistence that bodies do not ultimately matter will be the rationalization *a posteriori* or argument *a priori*: Humans have always been greater than the skin suits with which they were first provided; the body lets its owner down; it is the mind that makes one human, etc., etc.

Perhaps the preservation and/or augmentation of the humanoid system will someday fall out of fashion, and humans will accept without fear or shame their mechanization. If man knows what parts of his body will betray him and when, and he has the capacity to banish that part in advance and replace it with metal or plastic, with something synthetic, with something loyal, won't he do it? Won't he cast aside his inflamed liver, his sticky lungs, his leaky heart long before the swelling, the mucus, the skip-skip-skips? Man will see his death coming, and he will kill the killer inside of him first, swapping him out for clones with less carbon.

Baudrillard's problematic concept of deterrence works better here, a simulation of a thing to make the real thing impossible. In this case, it is a little death to stopgap Death death, expulsion to prevent expiration, cutting yourself into pieces to keep your pieces from getting to you first. We are already there—the rich and famous will and do cyborg themselves first, on the cover of *Vogue* (notable exceptions being the poor and veteran who undergo testing first) and in the *New York Times*. They are "brave," and they are brave.

Women, especially, can blow up the life raft before the boat leaves the harbor with precautionary hysterectomies and prophylactic mastectomies. She can cyborg herself some new boobs, or she can leave herself stripped like a tree in winter to remain bare when spring comes. Birch bark.

It is a good way to start our cyborgization. The doctors advised us to. We did it to save our lives. Better to be safe than sorry. Better to be less than too much. Less of you to kill you. We will not be seen as vain. We've been messing with our outsides to look better since the beginning, while simultaneously inhaling and ingesting junk. Preventative cyborgization will be for health reasons, which is code for immortality reasons. Death does not have to be a preexisting condition. Only your body can kill you. Who says this has to be your body?

Not that choosing not you isn't an extraordinary process and decision. You have to sacrifice to save. You are both Jesus and Lazarus. You bring yourself back from the dead. As Donna Haraway writes,

> To be One is to be autonomous, to be powerful, to be God; but to be One is to be an illusion, and so to be involved in a dialectic of apocalypse with the other. Yet to be other is to be multiple, without clear boundary, frayed, insubstantial. One is too few, but two are too many.[12]

If man is made in the image of God, as millions around the globe believe, and is not original material but modeled on something better, bigger—the origin story of the human species then is one of original unoriginality. Man is the first cheap knockoff, made like Edward Scissorhands to alleviate his Creator's loneliness. For the scientifically minded, the reasoning is not so different, but rather than an old man being a little vain and a little hungry for company, the (rather more expensive) knockoff is the biological impulse known as sexual reproduction. We copy ourselves to keep from being alone, which is the same as to keep from dying, and because on a basic level we're pretty into ourselves. We don't like some versions—in fact the more differences between us and another person, the more we tend to dislike him. We prefer people who share traits with us, though less so doppelgängers, clones, and impersonators; they freak us out, those impostors, those evil twins, as threatening to us as those who have no similarities. It is in neither of our best interests to keep us around when we are identical or when we are opposite.

When we cyborg ourselves, we remove ourselves from both ideological camps. No longer are we copies of what God or science has made. Some of the conditions that make us need transplants and prosthetics are heritable, but not all, and we typically have a choice about what to do with the deeply vulnerable bodies we are granted, a choice that was never given to us by our biology or our deities.

Where prosthesis and mechanization can provide options, however, it may also take them away. The Western idea that prosthetics give a person his or her independence back is not the same as the Soviet thought process. Individuality does not go with mechanization. According to Nicolas Sutil,

> Soviet workers were told that in order to produce the best trajectory for the hammering motion in the assembly line, the worker had to follow the quantified and exactly measured movement curves produced by mathematicians and scientists. . . . Where science objectified and instrumentalized the body and its physical intelligence, the political establishment in turn instrumentalized scientific knowledge for its own self-serving purposes.[13]

This, and Nikolay Chernyshevsky's belief that "movement is reality . . . because movement is life. But life has as its main element labor; consequently, the main element of reality is labor and the truest sign of reality is activity,"[14] acknowledges that, though motion does not make a person more or less real, more or less their own self, it is bad enough if it feels that way. While the paralyzed, in their broken shells, still retain the ghost, no motion is akin to coerced motion. The hobbling of the capacity for self-expression more than the loss of flesh or ability, or even freedom, is truly what cuts man off from his humanity. To have only a single path open to him will always seem as if to be trapped or dead. If we become too much machine, too much product rather than production, we may have too few options—or too many, an opposite but equal problem—open to us to still be "real" to ourselves (the only ones who really matter), to still have stories and lives we can call our own. As long as we are capable of living and dying in more than one way, we are contained within a system of both options and limitations. This is what it means to be alive, and thus "real." Movement is not reality; choice, in a framework, is.

6 DAVIDS

If our parts are replaceable, then eventually, if not already, so must be our wholes. In the West there is no greater terror than that of being replaced. Our value as individuals informs our friendships, our romantic relationships, our work lives, and our xenophobia. If we are not providing something unique, something special, in our relationships, the people in our lives might leave us—replace us with friends or loved ones who are more generous, less clingy, like vacuuming, won't make you go camping. If we are not by a combination of skills, personality, and experience the only ones who can do our jobs, then we may be let go—replaced with machines that don't make mistakes, have babies, or file workmen's comp.

The Western anxiety about being replaced is discussed most directly in music. In her song "Irreplaceable," Beyoncé is defiant. Beyoncé's ex is trying to convince her that he gives her something essential that no one else can. He is terrified, understandably, of losing Beyoncé, but she doesn't believe that his absence can't be filled by something equal or better. The chorus fittingly goes, "I could have another you in a minute/Matter fact he'll be here in a minute, baby," as it is the man's treatment of Beyoncé as replaceable—or, at least, insufficient to occupy the role of one and only—that led her to kick him out in the first place. "So since I'm not your everything/How about I'll be nothing, nothing at all to you/Baby I won't shed a tear for you/I won't lose a wink of sleep/'Cause the truth of the matter/Is replacing you is so easy." One gets the impression that Beyoncé may not believe what she is singing now, but is singing it to convince herself, like smiling until you're happy, as well as to win the break-up. When someone hurts you and your brain knows that the best thing to do is be rid of that person, but your heart isn't so sure, putting on a good show is paramount to ending the toxic relationship, and this punishment-cum-self-hypnosis is good for women to hear and emulate.

The problem implicit in this song and Western culture is that, while it is of the highest importance to Beyoncé to feel irreplaceable in relationships, she may also note that it is in her best interest to not set others up on such high a pedestal. To invest that fully in someone else is to tempt fate and can regularly lead to heartbreak. This need to achieve irreplaceability while never falling for it in another is of course wildly unhealthy and creates relationships that are entirely out of balance and unsustainable.

In the song "Afraid" by The Neighbourhood, an underappreciated British band, the lead singer is violently afraid of being found out, of the people in his life realizing he actually sucks and is easily replaced. "When I wake up I'm afraid, somebody else might take my place/When I wake up I'm afraid, somebody else might end up being me." If we don't matter to someone or something, then do we matter at all? Who are we if we are replaceable, forgettable, mortal long before we are dead?

Doppelgängers, impersonators, and clones are the most literal realizations of this fear of being replaced—people who look and act and even have the same genetic material threaten their source material with obsolescence. Where unnatural twins appear, we know to be afraid. In the collective imagination, only we can have our families, friends, jobs, and dreams. Two cannot occupy this highly specialized, individual space. If fake versions of ourselves come, they come not to share, but to depose, stealing our skin right off our bodies as they kick us from the thrones of our lives.

To assume the voice of

First used in the early 1600s, the word "impersonation" meant "to invest with a personality" and later "to assume the person or character of." The concept of impersonation has always enjoyed the sensation of fraud, and that perception continues to this day. Though what constitutes criminal impersonation in the United States varies by state, New York law is a good example. It states:

A person is guilty of criminal impersonation in the first degree when he:

1 Pretends to be a police officer or a federal law enforcement officer as enumerated in section 2.15 of the criminal procedure law, or wears or displays without authority, any uniform, badge or other insignia or facsimile thereof, by which such police officer or federal law enforcement officer is lawfully distinguished or expresses by his or her words or actions that he or she is acting with the approval or authority of any police department or acting as a federal law enforcement officer with the approval of any agency that employs federal law enforcement officers as enumerated in section 2.15 of the criminal procedure law; and

2 So acts with intent to induce another to submit to such pretended official authority or otherwise to act in reliance upon said pretense and in the course of such pretense commits or attempts to commit a felony; or

3 Pretending to be a duly licensed physician or other person authorized to issue a prescription for any drug or any instrument or device used in the taking or administering of drugs for which a prescription

is required by law, communicates to a pharmacist an oral prescription which is required to be reduced to writing pursuant to section thirty-three hundred thirty-two of the public health law.[1]

Capacity for and intent to commit harm are of primary importance in criminal impersonation. Capacity for harm depends not only on the importance of the work of the person being impersonated but—and this isn't written into the law—the skill and means to pull off the deception. If you're really good at impersonation, you don't get caught. If you're terrible (aka, drunk or joking around), no one takes you seriously; you can't even rise to the level of committing the crime. Only the people in the middle—people who are serious in the impersonation attempt but are not convincing for the necessary length of time—are the ones who end up on trial.

Rarely are remakes beloved, and Sydney Pollack's update of *Sabrina* is nearly universally panned. Though I loved it and could very well spend an entire chapter of this book proclaiming all its virtues, let me restrict myself to a single quote, from a fictional *Vogue France* editor named Irene (Fanny Ardant): "Illusions are dangerous people," Irene tells Sabrina (Julia Ormond), regarding the latter's unrequited crush on David Larrabee (Greg Kinnear). "They have no flaws."

Here we find the road forks sharply: on the left the sun-dappled path built by impressionists; on the right the gnarled, shadowy, goosebump-inducing trail maintained by impersonators down which so many visitors are reluctant to veer. For those of us unwilling to suspend disbelief, impersonators, in their attempts to ape the manufactured personas of celebrities, can seem downright creepy. Wearing rose-colored glasses, they sculpt perfect, shallow Davids, beautiful archetypes instead of unique individuals. Alternately, impressionists, to get back to my skin-stealing turn of phrase, aren't trying to step into poreless, marble-like skin, but to magnify the zit of the person and mock it for all its worth.

In pursuit of a moment and a laugh, impressionists exaggerate the crack in a celebrity's public persona in order to achieve something closer to the actual human in the celebrity, something that feels more deserving of the term "tribute." Impersonators, on the other hand, do not exaggerate; they value authenticity, though often the authenticity of the *persona* rather than the person. In the documentary *Just About Famous*, Betty Atchison, who impersonates Lady Gaga, talks about rising above "party store lookalikes" (people who just buy a costume), differentiating herself from lesser impersonators. "A lookalike on stage without dancers," Atchison clarifies, "is sort of glorified karaoke."

"To really perform as that character," Atchison continues, "you've got to take it to as high a level and high a quality as you can. And to be as authentic as you can, not just the look, but also the voice, the walk, the talk, and the music, and the dance." Reality for Atchison, the reality of Lady Gaga, is in the performance. Or, as our old frenemy Ada Louise

Huxtable says in *Unreal America*, "Identity is a product of the mood and the moment; the persona is the clothes that hang in the closet."[2] Identity is internal; persona external. The impersonator focuses on the persona; the impressionist on the identity.

This choice is akin to that of wax museums, which also replicate the celluloid or image of the celebrity rather than his or her humanity. The wax figures don't look quite right, all smoothed out as if Photoshopped—so close to real it's unnatural, disturbing. Perhaps it's that the impersonator, like the wax figure, by trying to imitate the persona and so often conflating character with actor or singer, seems to trap a real person in a surreal iteration of it. Instead of body-snatching, however, wax figures have snatched personas and then crystallized them in a barely figurative amber.

Though celebrity impersonation can be divided, messily, into two kinds of impersonators—people who impersonate celebrities and people who impersonate characters made famous by celebrities (a nesting doll choice not dissimilar to amusement parks based on movies)—there is some overlap, as celebrity and character can be indistinguishable. In addition, impersonators are known to take on the roles of people that require an extra level of suspending disbelief, specifically when they choose to impersonate a dead person (like Elvis or Marilyn Monroe) or a younger version of a living celebrity (like Madonna).

The documentary I mentioned above, *Just About Famous*, which interviews celebrity impersonators at a convention in

Orlando, Florida, attempts to show that impersonators are aware they are doing a job and not forgetting who they really are. But identity crisis at the level of madness and identity crisis at the level of dissatisfaction with the realities of one's non-impersonation life are two very different things, and the latter most certainly applies to many of the impersonators, whose jobs are more than jobs, for better or worse.

"As much as I enjoy the impersonation, I'm looking for the opportunity to be real," says John Morgan, the George W. Bush impersonator. "There's a part of me that wants to now kind of launch into this new phase of my career where I am a motivator who impersonates George Bush rather than a George Bush impersonator who sings and that's all there is."

Sean Banks, a Barack Obama impersonator, is similarly not quite satisfied with just pretending to be an accomplished politician. In fact, as is regularly the case, art inspires life, and Banks starts to think about running for public office in Florida. When he tells this to an actual politician, Chris Nabicht, a candidate for the Deltona City Commission, Nabicht has these words of wisdom for Banks: "If, you know, you rely on somebody else's image, you're gonna be stuck with some of their baggage. Be your own man, but you're gonna run your own game. You don't need to rely on ridin' on somebody else's coattails." Later, when Banks walks around his neighborhood trying to get signatures for the petition that will let him be on the ballot in November, he does far better when he walks around as himself rather than as Obama.

By the end of the documentary, however, Banks has decided not to run for public office but to work behind the scenes, having been elected the president of the Democratic Club of Southwest Volusia County. Here the cameraman shows footage of Banks slipping a name tag in a badge holder; on closer inspection the badge looks like a fake. The name on it is Sean Ngying, which turns out to be Sean's real name, and both Democratic and President are spelled incorrectly (Democrate and Pesident respectively). Is Sean's political journey, as told to us, legitimate? When impersonators spend so much time pretending to be someone else, does this bleed into the rest of their lives?

Though most of us are more comfortable with the impression over the impersonation, impressions are strange inventions as well. Within the concept of the impression is the idea that people are reducible. Consider the sheer volume of Matthew McConaughey, Christopher Walken, Al Pacino, Robert De Niro, Marlon Brando, and Sean Connery impressions. Just about every English-speaking man and a heck of a lot of women think they can do serviceable imitations of at least one, if not all, of these actors. Yes, they are very famous men, but they aren't necessarily the most famous. Something in their voices and behaviors is both easy to identify and easy to replicate *sans* makeup or costume. As such, a major part of these actors, the part of themselves they make visible to the world in every role, and so, we assume, the part that carries over to their "real lives," is now so frequently copied *with frontloaded attribution* that it actually serves to help make the actors immortal. The intonations and accents, speech patterns, hand gestures, squints and smiles—they now exclusively belong to those celebrities who are reduced to performative synecdoche. These famous men's exaggerated qualities, from the Brando chin scratch and the De Niro mugging to the McConaughey drawl and the measured Walken diction, may very well outlast the art that made their impressionists pay such close attention.

Klone

Not being Jewish, my first encounter with the golem was in Michael Chabon's *The Amazing Adventures of Kavalier & Clay*. The phrasing of man being formed from clay finds in the golem its most literal realization and rotates him back to his mythological proto-self—this is the ontology of golems, automatons, and Frankenstein's creature that separates them from cyborgs: that not just the shape of man, but the man-ness of man, is makeable. Beyond the mannequin stretching in the store window or the sculpture holed up in a museum alcove, beyond mechanical engineering and robotics, we can by magic (in stories) or science (in the plausible future) do what only the divine/nature has been able to do beforehand—Create with a capital C.

The closest we have come is with human cloning. After Dolly the sheep was cloned in 1996, many nations passed laws preventing any human cloning—but not all of them. In

1998 American biotech company Advanced Cell Technology (now known as Ocata Therapeutics, Inc.) created the first hybrid human clone through somatic cell nuclear transfer (SCNT). After the nucleus from a man's leg cell was implanted into a cow's egg from which the nucleus had been removed, the hybrid cell was cultured and developed into an embryo. Twelve days later it was destroyed.[3]

Hand in hand with stem cell research, therapeutic cloning research has advanced far past SCNT, but is still, as of this writing, not used in medical practice anywhere. Many countries have banned any work in this field due to fears that therapeutic cloning can't help but lead to the other side of human cloning that not a single nation has expressly legalized: reproductive cloning, aka, the cloning at the black heart of some of our scarier science-fiction works (as well as Harold Ramis's *Multiplicity*, which could be accused of other human rights violations).

People of all backgrounds have reasons for being against this kind of research. When life begins and what collection of atoms constitutes life remains a thorny issue for many religious groups, particularly Catholics, which throws a big red X on embryonic stem cell research. In addition, the morally questionable and physically bloody ends such research could lead to (like clone organ farming, the subject behind—spoiler alert—Kazuo Ishiguro's novel *Never Let Me Go*) is what lies at the bottom of the therapeutic cloning bunny slope for the politicians, scientists, and human rights activists who argue for strict regulation or complete bans of global cloning research. For the general public, however, the concern has never seemed to be on behalf of the clones and their possible exploitation, and yet in practical terms cloning is far more likely to lead to the abuse of clones, of creating bodies not for experiencing life but for sustaining organs for the individuals who provided the genetic material. Rather, the public at large imagines clones are junior versions of themselves, slowly growing unsatisfied with second-class citizenhood, regardless of the actual degree of oppression. But equality (at least theoretically) is not hard to grant and nothing to fear. If people fear clones, then they must do so because they imagine clones, like the proverbial machines, will rise up—not to live side by side with their forbears, but to eliminate them. Where does this idea, that one might so resent being a Xerox as to destroy the original document, come from? It would make sense if our species identified strongly with fermions, particles, which, if identical, cannot occupy the same quantum state within a quantum system at the same time. But, last time I checked, people aren't overly inclined to anthropomorphize principles in quantum physics. The fear instead seems to generate from the same place issue I've noted throughout this book—the idea that to be a copy is to not be real and thus inherently bad. Even the Council of Europe, by referring to the "need to respect the human being both as an individual and as a member of the human species" in its 1997 Convention on Human Rights with Regard to Biomedicine, seems to back this idea that cloning could be a threat to self-identification.

Even within a group, identity is wrapped up in our individuality. I am a member of this family, this organization, this community, but I have a role in this family, organization, or community that makes me indispensable, that makes me unique, that makes me elemental. A younger, potentially better copy of me is a threat to my place in the world, to my very life. Even if doppelgängers in fiction don't have evil intentions, protagonists often attribute sinister motives to the doppelgänger regardless and try to eliminate the imitator before it can take over his life, either by destroying his corporeal form or by taking his relationships, possessions, and identity from him (regardless of whether the doppelgänger desires to or not). Twins do not seem to have this problem, though you wouldn't think so from the number of times the antagonist in fiction turns out to be someone's "evil twin." People are narcissists—they are obsessed with what they see in the mirror. But unless they see their clone/doppelgänger/twin as not just family, but as *part* of their identity, rather than a menace to it, they are as distrustful of it as those aphasiacs who try to throw their own legs out of bed, thinking the leg doesn't belong to them.

And the fear is not simply of being replaced, but of questioning one's own reality, of one's own identity. Only I am I. Only I am real. But, as with the fear of humanoid robots, the worry is not, at the event of the singularity, that the robots or clones will destroy us so much as it is they will destroy our ability to know ourselves, to identify ourselves as "real," as human, as not-clone, not-robot. How will we know that we were not programmed to believe otherwise, that we were not created by scientists in a lab, that we came first, that we are who we think we are, that our thoughts and stories are what we know them to be? How will we be sure of anything if persona and identity are indistinguishable? *Blade Runner* is not just a movie, after all; it is a philosophical treatise that is continually being rewritten.

> Late twentieth-century machines have made thoroughly ambiguous the difference between natural and artificial, mind and body, self-developing and externally designed, and many other distinctions that used to apply to organisms and machines. Our machines are disturbingly lovely, and we ourselves frighteningly inert.[4]

Our anticipations of that which robotics and cloning are capable are swaddled in what we believe the human race is capable of generating—its own destruction through its obsession with developing that divinity skill—but our imaginings about the end results of our imagination are not outside the realm of possibility. And it also explains why we can both be impressed by impressionists who exaggerate and mock the individual, but fear and despise impersonators the more they impress us. Impersonators are scratch pad doppelgängers. They take away knowing what is "real," or where we orient ourselves, in our bodies, our memories, our situation in time and place—our exeroceptive and proprioceptive senses may fail us at any moment.

Virtual reality takes this further, though it doesn't feel that way, in that it clones place and experience but lets us retain control. If virtual reality hadn't been preceded by theme parks and video games, if it wasn't currently being marketed as entertainment, we would be as terrified of it as we are of cloning. There have been warning stories of getting lost in virtual reality, not to mention *The Matrix* and its depiction of virtual reality as a tool of sedation, but it is nothing inherent in the virtual reality that is dangerous, only the programmers and users. For clones and robots, the opposite is the case— we don't believe the engineers and scientists who Create can control their Creations any more than God has been able to reign us in. We don't trust clones or robots because we have met ourselves, and there is no reason to think anything made in our image would be better than us. The golem might be a hero, but in the end is far more likely to be a monster.

As the second decade of the twenty-first century winds down, however, criminal impersonation is enough to be upset about. Bots, programs pretending to be online humans, troll our digital lives to influence the socioeconomic and political landscape—and do so to great effect. Despite fretting about our imminent replacement and takeover by computers for decades, we struggle to acknowledge that it is already happening. Non-violent and restricted to the Internet, we didn't need the singularity to be impersonated or cloned. Since our voices are where, like the Little Mermaid, our power rests, this is the only part of ourselves technology ever needed or will need to steal from us. We should have seen it coming long ago. From bots back to catfishing—a practice utilized by both sexual predators and teens low in self-confidence—back to old-school impersonators and impressionists, to capture the nucleus of personhood a thief has always first targeted his victim's voice. Since we are nothing *but* voices in our Internet lives, this priority, rather than being primary, is now singular. Our voices, which we thought beautiful, unique, and inimitable, have turned out to be our greatest weaknesses.

γνῶθι σεαυτόν[*]

If you are what you eat and wear, the places you live and visit, your relationships and your very organs, and if fakeness is infiltrating all those aspects of your world, it is natural to suspect that the fakeness is contagious and at some point you too will become fake, that you won't be able to help it, and that you might not be able to stop it when it happens—or even know that it is happening.

Everyone is a composite of the internal and external, and it is paradoxically because of this commonality that no one thing manages to affect each of us in the same way; even plagues don't wipe everyone out. Our differences may be the one struggle humanity cannot overcome, but those differences are

---

[*] "Know thyself" in Greek.

also what keep us alive as a species. Our ability to distinguish between reality and virtual reality, men and their wannabes, seems like an important one. Beyond homophobia, this is why some have lingering fears or anxieties about those in the trans community. They fear being tricked; they want disclosure about what body the person was born into, seeing that original flesh as the "real" or "true" person, and the new body a fraud being perpetrated upon unsuspecting folks. They have this switched, however. The "natural" body, the body the trans person was born into, this is the fake, as foreign and wrong as a tumor (which is also "natural" and can form in the womb), and the playacting was what was going on *before* gender reassignment, not after. To identify as trans, to live as the person you are inside, is to choose truth, as difficult as it might be for the rest of the world to perceive.

"Know thyself." "To thine own self be true." These seemingly simple old adages are anything but. To really know oneself, to come to terms with one's identity, is an ongoing process more difficult than almost any in which humans engage. People are stuck with themselves and take on all manner of activities, both life-threatening and benign, to pretend they are not. They can only ignore who they are for so long, however, and eventually must confront themselves. Individuals can change and grow, but everyone has a core self that is theoretically immutable. As Donna Haraway said, "we don't need organic holism to give impermeable wholeness."[5] That completeness, that realness, rests in the core self.

I wish that core self was invulnerable, but what happens to aphasiacs—those with lesions on their brains that irreparably warp their perception of both themselves and the world—would suggest otherwise; man is only what his brain says he is. No clones will be different—they too will be governed entirely by their brains. If they think, they are, trapped by what their neurons or wires tell them, delusion or otherwise. This is the degradation we cannot prevent, excuse, or fix by transplant or prosthetic. Though it is rare, it is the only true way we can be rendered untrue to ourselves—by no longer knowing who that self is.

7 OVID AND THE REAL GIRL

There is another kind of "fake" person, one we haven't talked about yet. This is the relationship "proxy," so called because it serves as a substitute for a consensual, non-monetary relationship between two people. Relationship proxies are ubiquitous in the modern world, in such forms as pets, nannies, psychiatrists, and so on, but for the purposes of this little black dress of a chapter let's focus on the romantic and sexual relationship proxies, which are numerous in their own right. The romantic proxy typically begins with a straight-up lie—the "boyfriend from summer camp who lives in Canada"—and may stop there. For heterosexual women, the romantic and sexual proxy is often limited to figments of the imagination, while men have far more options—prostitutes, gigolos, call girls, girlfriend experiences, sex dolls, and (though it's still in its infancy) sex robots. Yes, women can hire men for sex as well, but the market is not for or about women—it's for men, particularly heterosexual cisgender men.

Despite the feminist battle against it, much of a woman's life is still spent fighting the mirror and the shopping mall. To get laid, a woman must dehumanize herself, make herself less animal and more clean, chemical, machine or doll—remove hair, add color, stop eating, learn the codes, work out the bugs. She is still taught that a substitute self, a model of herself, is the only way to catch and keep a "real man." But "real men" are also a tricky blueprint to read—"real men" are gentleman feminists who hunt and fuck but also listen and cook. "Real men" are strong, silent types, who also know how to express their feelings. "Real men" are Bruce Wayne if he went to therapy, James Bond if he wasn't such a womanizer, Jon Hamm on that episode of *2 Dope Queens**—woke but also funny but not "on" all the time but strong but not a gym rat but handsome but not shallow but smart but not a know-it-all but not gropey but but but.

In *Lars and the Real Girl*, Lars (Ryan Gosling) has a girlfriend who is real to him in the only ways with which he is equipped to engage. She is less a sex doll than a blow-up girlfriend experience. Sometimes it is not sex that can't handle us, but we who can't handle sex. Or, in Lars's case, the people who come with the sex. Humans are hard, ourselves most of all, and the benefit of dolls or sex workers is not only that they provide sex without the same kind of

---

*Haven't heard it? Go find it and listen to it. The book will wait. Not forever, but a couple hours, yes.

messiness inherent in non-transactional, human-to-human relationships, but that their continued presence and affection is not dependent upon compliance with social niceties people like Lars may find difficult to achieve.

While certainly some heterosexual cisgender women have moral or religious stances against prostitution and sex dolls, and others are simply afraid of losing their existing or future partners, the most egregious problem of relationship and sex proxies is this inequity for those women who, despite the common assumption, "can't just go out and get sex whenever they want" or want to pay for a boyfriend experience they control. The fact that these women are restricted in what side they can be on in transactional sex is the most un-feminist part of prostitution.[*]

Yes, plenty of sex toys are available for women to purchase. One could argue that sex dolls and robots are not, in fact, relationship proxies, and the difference is that men have sex with a woman's whole body while women only have sex with the man's phallus, blah blah blah. But dildos and vibrators are never indistinguishable from a relationship proxy. As much as a woman may like her sex toy, may even be addicted to it and use it as a substitute for sex with other people, she does not mistake it for a person or a relationship. There is no *Lars and the Real Girl* about a woman and her Rabbit, not in fiction and not in real life.

---

[*] Though . . . also, pimps.

What sex toys and relationship proxies, of varieties both animate and in-, do have in common is that by demanding nothing of the customer but legal tender, their so-called inauthenticity allows the customer to be himself, to be authentic. He does not have to cyborg himself, try to trick the prostitute or phallus into fucking or loving him—he has paid with cash instead of his identity.

That is important. Sex toys and relationship proxies can be candy, but they can also be medicine, dangerously difficult for the judgmental to differentiate. Monogamous, long-term relationships no longer have to suffer when one partner does not have the physical desire or ability to satisfy the other's sexual needs. Trauma victims can take baby steps. People who want to get off can get off without having to sell themselves in all the myriad ways a person can sell herself. Like stunt doubles, sex toys and relationship proxies aren't necessarily stealing "real" people's jobs; sometimes they're just helping out.

The most intimate moment between two people is also the one with which humans have been dissatisfied for not just all of recorded history, but before it, too. Considering "the vaginal insertion of objects for sexual pleasure has been observed among primates in the wild,[1]" probably before humans were even "humans."

Not only were our ancestors dissatisfied with the basics, they were weird about it, too. From the artifacts, parietal paintings, and oral histories that make up the sum of ancient human history, anthropologists and archaeologists have posited that many past civilizations performed fertility ceremonies and rituals in which the symbolic was inseparable from reality. Fertility was a matter of more than just the man and woman engaged in coitus; having sex to produce children was also a matter for ancestral spirits, gods of various forms, the elders of the tribe, and the natural world around them. The male genitalia was the magic wand wielded by these great forces to bring forth life from the woman's belly, a place of as much mystery and power as the penis that inspired it to fruition. Without the blessings of the environment and the gods, without the right sacrifice, prayer, or offering, the magic of the sexual act would not catalyze. Simulations of sex and birth may have had value for preserving memory or ritual, and phallic objects, such as the *bâtons de commandements* found in caves like Les Trois Freres, may have had any number of purposes, but nothing about the performance was more or less "fake" than actual copulation. To this day, sex is never "just" sex. Whether to produce a child, achieve or give pleasure, as part of a ritual, to display power or prove value, sex always has purpose.

The half-human, half-something-elses that fill mythology all got that way because their mothers or fathers copulated with non-persons, be they god, beast, plant, or element. While all of these hybrid origin stories may have been backtracking to explain the strange beings of our imaginations, ancient peoples decided that extra-human capacity to take on the world—powers, as it were—could only be achieved through intimacy with those who were not human, and while some hybrids were monsters (the Minotaur), others were heroes (Hercules, Jesus).

If the human body has been cyborg for some time and is only becoming more so, it's unsurprising that so too have human relationships. Though procreation no longer requires sex, copulation ostensibly remains the cheapest way of getting the job done—if not necessarily the easiest. When Aziz Ansari refers to Tokyo's high incidence of sex toys, hostess clubs, and other ways of paying for attention and affection as a "'relationship replacement' industry"[2] in his book *Modern Romance*, it's important not to be sucked into the hyperbolic whirlpool. The idea I want us to focus on here is not that Japanese men are destroying the birthrate in their country because they're afraid of women or that the market is keeping them from ever being too lonely or desperate to date in the traditional sense. It's this two-part question:

What makes sexual or romantic experiences or activities "replacements" for what have been heretofore known as "real" relationships, and will such supposed "fake" relationships herald forth or be emblematic of the end times? The modern-day line of reasoning seems to go: too much time on computers >>> online or virtual relationships >>> social anxiety when it comes to face-to-face interactions >>> capitalism >>> monetary exchange for affection, attention, protection from rejection and/or commitment >>> fewer long-term relationships and less sex outside of professional interactions >>> low marriage and birth rate.

Western society has taken capitalism into its loving arms and yet, while holding it so close, regards it as the great instigator of inauthenticity. The sense seems to be that the instant capitalism breaks free of that warm embrace, it is bound to stab society in the back with a cheap knife it got off Amazon. But while capitalism is indeed not to be trusted outside regulation's restrictive embrace, injecting aboveboard capitalism into a relationship does not denature the reality of that relationship. Since sex is and always has been inseparable from exchange, why should the act of buying sex mean you are not having a relationship with the person from whom you are buying sex? Because the assumption is that one party is only pretending to enjoy oneself? It doesn't matter if she actually is or is not; as soon as she was given money to have sex, the possible sexual or romantic relationship became a client-service relationship, but an emotional experience of some kind is still happening for at least one member of the party. There is nothing proxy about a relationship just because the feelings may be one-sided. That is a risk anyone in any kind of relationship must face.

If people despise relationship proxies, they do so in the same way they despise clones: fear of being replaced and shame of their curiosity at the idea of officially commodifying what, in the best of all possible worlds, would be given and taken freely and without complication or worry about being punished for the sin of taking the nature out of love and sex and replacing it with plastic.

Yet while prostitutes may take men away from women with other professions, prostitutes do not steal the faces of those they are replacing. Where impersonators and clones further intersect with blow-up dolls and robots, of course, is that they have this capacity—that at some point your image may be replicated, in one way or another, and your choices about how your image is used stolen from you. Your image may engage, by choice or force, in activities about which you have no say or control. Identity theft dupes the audience, but it also slanders the person whose identity is stolen. It misattributes violently. It takes away a person's right to her public persona.

When people talk about living in a bubble, either for others or themselves, they are deluding themselves. No one, not even people who live in actual medical bubbles, lives in a bubble. Not one of us has total control over any single aspect of our lives—not our health, not our education, not our finances, not our careers, not our family, not our friendships, not our romantic or sex lives (unfortunately), and certainly not how we are viewed by others. All relationships require a suspension of disbelief. In standard, socially accepted relationships we refer to that suspension as "faith" or "trust." We can give love a go and hope that our relationships are with people who are exactly who they claim to be, but we are locked inside ourselves for better or worse, and our ability to get inside others' brains is severely limited. We barely know our own.

*　　*　　*

Which brings us to orgasm. Excuse me. Which brings us to *the* orgasm.

In her autobiography *The Book of Love*, Meg Ryan recounts what director Rob Reiner told her before the infamous scene where she verbalizes a sandwich-stimulated orgasm:

> If the art which I so long have practised has aught of worth in it, then list to me; my words will not deceive you. So, then, my dear ones, feel the pleasure in the very marrow of your bones; share it fairly with your lover, say pleasant, naughty things the while.
>
> And if Nature has withheld from you the sensation of pleasure, then teach your lips to lie and say you feel it all. Unhappy is the woman who feels no answering thrill. But, if you have to pretend, don't betray yourself by over-acting. Let your movements and your eyes combine to deceive us, and, gasping, panting, complete the illusion.[3]

Apologies again. Meg Ryan wrote no such book, and Rob Reiner said no such thing. In actuality, the above quote is from Jesus's contemporary, the Roman poet Ovid, in his instruction manual for quenching your thirst, *Ars Amatoria*, or *The Art of Love*.

Long before *When Harry Met Sally* placed "faking it" into the cultural zeitgeist, Ovid was handing out all kinds of advice on duping lovers. Take for example:

> If you want to keep your mistress's love, you must make her think you're dazzled with her charms. If she wears a dress of Tyrian purple, tell her there's nothing like Tyrian purple. . . . Be a good dissembler and never let your face belie your words. Artifice is a fine thing when it's not perceived; once it's discovered, discomfiture follows. Confidence is gone for ever.[4]

Strangely, before Ovid suggested men lie a little for their lovers' sake and also instructed women on how to feign seeing the face of Jupiter when all they saw was the face of Vulcan, he wrote in the same text,

> I hate a woman who offers herself because she ought to do so, and, cold and dry, thinks of her sewing when she's making love. The pleasure that is granted to me from a sense of duty ceases to be a pleasure at all. I won't have any woman doing her duty towards me.

as well as,

> Take heed lest, cramming on too much sail, you speed too swiftly for your mistress. Nor should you suffer her to outstrip you. Speed on together towards the promised

haven. The height of bliss is reached when, unable any longer to withstand the wave of pleasure, lover and mistress at one and the same moment are overcome. Such should be thy rule when time is yours and fear does not compel you to hasten your stolen pleasures. Nevertheless, if there be danger in delay, lean well forward, and drive your spur deep into your courser's side.

The fake orgasm ideally should be the last recourse, because in a heterosexual coupling, Ovid believed, both partners should get off, preferably together—mutual gratification then, not impregnation, being the goal of the sexual act.

Two thousand years later, it's hard to imagine a heterosexual man stating that he only wants to have sex with women who are really into it in the same text where he also advises them to just go for the semblance of orgasm . . basically, to be a good sport.

If Timothy Taylor is right that "faking orgasm, like developed language, is apparently unique to humans"[5]—it's not really something we can say for certain, as there are other ways outside of language to simulate orgasm—then people do indeed beat out elephants and whales in the empathy games because they are the only creatures who logic their concern for another into deceit.

While it's certainly polite to "fake it," gratifying a partner in bed may be both a great sacrificial act of love and the death of it. To declaim orgasm is to mask the reality of one's sexual experience. If honest communication is the key to a relationship, the casual lies suggested by Ovid two millennia ago and depicted in so many fictional portraits of marriage today serves to corrode the cuts on that key's blade. "Faking it" in sex may seem like you're putting your partner's needs ahead of your own or protecting his (or even her) feelings, but what is really happening is that the emotional nakedness so important to romantic sex is being obstructed. Anxieties are compiled, insecurities buried and fertilized, and desires shelved.

Why is it so hard to be honest in bed? Because to be dissatisfied or understimulated by a partner can be seen or felt as betrayal, as insufficient love.

This is, of course, ridiculous. The basic package doesn't come with HBO. If you want the premium shit, you have to ask for it (okay, that metaphor isn't perfect, because the cable companies absolutely try to sell you on the most expensive packages, but you get what I'm saying about upgrading).

So why am I down on *this* fake, and not so many of the others heretofore mentioned? Silk flowers, tofurkey, prosthetic legs, and silicone implants—a fake is not a fake unless it is a fraud, and these items, with the exception of some intentionally mislabeled foods, are not frauds. All the other purported proxies we have discussed here, whether for a penis, vagina, or relationship, are upfront about their limits, their un-"realness." Faking an orgasm, however, occurs within a non-transactional, human-to-human sexual encounter. It is perpetrating fraud, and it's causing the person committing the crime as much harm as the person being misled.

Do not fake orgasms, ladies—and men. If you do not like Tyrian purple, don't act as if you do. Communicate for the sake of your relationships. Be courageous; love yourselves; love your partners enough to let them rise to your satisfaction. Or get a proxy. It's more real than a dishonest orgasm.

8 THE START OF SOMETHING FAKE, PART 2

According to a study in the *International Journal of Behavioral Science*,[1] approximately 70 percent of people will struggle with "impostor syndrome" at least once in their lives. They will look at themselves, their circumstances, their accomplishments, their place in the world, and they will not believe all the evidence. They will see something in themselves that they do not recognize as possible, let alone true. Scientists do not consider this a psychological disorder; they consider it normal. The reality is, life is hard, and when something goes right, when you succeed, it feels too good to be true. Whether you thought you deserved the promotion or award or book contract before you received it is beside the point. Once you have the thing you worked so hard for, once you achieve what was kept from you, it's hard to just accept it. You don't want to be naïve; you don't want to be blindsided. People are conditioned to put their fingers in their ears, shut their eyes, and hum away the things that scare and worry them most, but also the things that make them most happy. Man trusts balance alone, and though that is what the universe is striving toward, it has no more achieved it than the rest of us.

For better or worse, all matter is. In *Lab Girl*, botanist Hope Jahren writes about discovering that the pit of a hackberry seed is made up of opal. Before she figured that out, no one knew it. We don't know everything about anything, not about the simple hackberry tree, not about even the items that we manufacture. Once Windex or Cheerios or this book leaves its maker's hands, new applications arise, target demographics change, unexpected toxic reactions occur, and the book lives a life I cannot predict. Living creatures are all just periodic tables rearranged—unstable, reactive, ever changing, ever bonding, and interacting and evolving. Inorganic materials fuse into something organic. A thing cannot be called fake or authentic, faux or real, imitation or genuine, not true or true, unless the person who calls it thus knows everything about the object and, when applicable, its maker, what the object is made of, what its creator intended for the object, what its creator did not intend for the object but accidentally designed into it, how all people will interact with the object, how the object will interact with the environment, and how it will change or be changed by the object to which it is paying structural or figurative homage. To determine the value of a thing in this way is to claim not only God-like comprehension of both past and present, but also the ability to see a future that hasn't been built yet.

I do not pretend that the net effect of "fakes" is necessarily positive. While man might be preventing further deforestation and extinction with fake flowers, faux fur, and soy burgers, he also created objects that do not break down quite so easily, objects outside of the cycle of life and death and decomposition. By creating implants and prosthetics to replace inadequate human body parts, he has improved the quality and length of life, yet also overstuffed the planet with billions of people it cannot easily support. And while one can defend museums, theme parks, restored ruins, and virtual realities as providing us with entrance into worlds man could never otherwise enter due to all kinds of temporal, spatial, financial, and environmental limits, one can also argue that escapism has reached peak saturation and that man continues to distract himself from the world's legitimate present-day problems at his peril.

What I have tried to express in the preceding chapters in another time would have seemed so indisputable and obvious as to be unworthy of a book, but this argument—that good versus bad, real versus fake, expensive versus cheap, and what I like versus what I don't like are not synonymous battles—has never felt more essential.

In the maybe-fake documentary *Exit Through the Gift Shop*, artist Shepard Fairey, discussing the work of Thierry Guetta aka Mr. Brainwash, says, "The more stickers that are out there, the more important it seems. The more important it seems, the more people want to know what it is, the more they ask each other, and it gains real power from perceived power." For much of what happens in our lives, this holds true for reality and truth as well—perceived reality and perceived truth become real reality and real truth—until un-perceived reality and truth intervene.

For too long now truth and reality have been defiled. Though reality did not run away, neither did it shake off the mud slung on it by pretenders to the throne. Somehow, and worse, the truth has found itself on equal footing with rumors, innuendos, gossip, and straight-up lies. All sound bites, all articles, all blogs, all memes possess the same weight, regardless of the level of fact-checking behind them. And when people call bullshit on misinformation, instead of the authors of the lies admitting or denying their guilt, they counterattack, volleying back the term "fake" without shame. "Fake" no longer appears to mean "not true"; it has turned into a label to attach to anything the other side says that the speaker does not like. The word has lost the power it was born with and gained a new, cancerous one. And as it has, truth and falsehood stare dead-eyed at each other on opposite ends of the seesaw, neither able to touch the earth nor the heavens.

In a 2005 episode of *The West Wing* written by Bradley Whitford, well before Barack Obama was campaigning for the presidency, Matt Santos (Jimmy Smits) concludes the episode with his own campaign announcement. At the end of his speech he says, "We live in cynical times, I know that. But hope is not up for debate. There is such a thing as false science, there is such a thing as false promises, and I am sure

I will have my share of false starts. But there is no such thing as false hope. There is only hope."

This phrasing seems prophetic of the two guiding principles that have followed the presidents to take over the actual West Wing since: one of hope, one of falseness.

Man can submit to any mass self-deception for a little while, but there are events so big that even our stubborn idiocy will crack beneath them. Unfortunately, these events are disasters—famine, drought, floods, fires, nuclear war. You can't troll the weather. You can't deny your way out of rising seas. And there is no lie that can make us turn our eyes the moment we're blown to smithereens.

People shouldn't have to lose their homes or their lives to understand that they can't hide under the covers from the things they fear and chant, "I don't believe," hoping reality will just go away.

Whether we are religious, spiritual, agnostic, or atheist, we are all very real humans sharing one planet, and we are failing our responsibilities to each other as a species and to the Earth as our home in very specific but fixable ways. The beginning of being better starts within, by breaking down our perceptions dispassionately and devil's advocating the tenets that make up our belief systems.

We are what make things, places, and each other "fake," and it is only we who, by being candid and curious, by looking not only at how we consume information but how we frame it, disseminate it, and alter it ourselves, by being unafraid to admit mistakes and hungry to educate ourselves so our mistakes aren't repeated, and by acknowledging our real, flawed humanity AND understanding that, as always, the status quo is just a place to start, can save each other and our common home from the tyranny of the unreal and untrue, from mutually assured destruction—from, ultimately, ourselves.

ACKNOWLEDGMENTS

Whatever demon was whispering into Christopher Schaberg's ear, first off, you've been derelict in your duties for the last thirty-odd years, and second, bless your devilish little heart. Now go talk in some other wise and powerful ears, you no-good sluggard (j/k, love you, mean it). Chris, Katherine, Augusta, Ian, and Haaris, thanks for letting me in your club.

This book could not have been written without libraries, specifically the University Library at American University in Washington, DC (you're the best, Adam), the Wallingford Public Library in Wallingford, CT, the Arlington Central Library in Arlington, VA, and the incomparable Library of Congress. If you are not using your local public library, you are a putz. They have FREE BOOKS! It's like Halloween all year, but you don't have to dress up or be a child, and instead of chocolate you get BOOKS! Seriously, whoever invented libraries should be on all the stamps.

If everyone judges this book by its cover, designed by genius Alice Marwick, I will count myself very lucky. When it comes to the innards, Susan, Leela, and James acted as my literary crime scene clean-up crew, for which I am bloody grateful.

Much gratitude to Allan Needell at the National Air and Space Museum, who answered my questions, and to the Smithsonian in general.

Cara Wolfe Jones, I am deeply thankful for your digital red pen and friendship of over twenty years. You can decide the order.

To my Sheehan, Yale, LA, Peace Corps China, and DC friends, thank you for being too numerous to name in these acknowledgments. I am #agnosticblessed to have had your support all these years. If you for one minute doubted my authorial abilities, you are the greatest fakers of all, because I never suspected your faith in me was anything but genuine.

To my family, especially Mom, Jerry, Allison, and Michelle, I love you like whoa. That's how you spell "whoa," everyone. Not "woah." Sorry for interrupting your acknowledgment with a spelling lesson, but you knew what you were getting when you kept me. You are my heartwood, and I would bear neither fruit nor flower without you with me.

Any errors in this book were totally intentional. I was just testing you, you passed, and, if you ever see me in the street, just give me a knowing nod. It'll be, like, *our thing*.

And finally, thanks to Idris Elba, just in case.

NOTES

Chapter 1

1   "Phony," Merriam-Webster.com, https://www.merriam-webster.com/dictionary/phony (accessed August 26, 2017).

2   William Shakespeare, *The Family Shakspeare,* ed. Thomas Bowdler (Philadelphia: J. W. Moore, 1849), v.

3   Shakespeare, *The Family Shakspeare,* v.

Chapter 2

1   Perry Walton, *The Story of Textiles* (Boston: J. S. Lawrence, 1912), 28.

2   "Fakes in Furs," *Cecil Whig,* April 2, 1904, http://chroniclingamerica.loc.gov/lccn/sn83016348/1904-04-02/ed-1/seq-7/ (accessed August 26, 2107).

3   Alice Hines, "The History of Faux Fur," *Smithsonian.com,* January 22, 2015, http://www.smithsonianmag.com/history/history-faux-fur-180953984/.

4 Anne Rittenhouse, "Furs Should Be Unattached," *Evening Star*, September 1, 1920, http://chroniclingamerica.loc.gov/lccn/sn83045462/1920-09-01/ed-1/seq-23/ (accessed August 26, 2017).

5 Wayne Pacelle, "Buyer Beware: Kohl's Selling Real Fur Advertised as Faux," *A Human(e) Nation*, December 2, 2013, http://blog.humanesociety.org/wayne/2013/12/kohls-selling-real-fur-advertised-as-faux.html.

6 Lindsay Deutsch, "Kohl's sorry faux fur on jacket was real raccoon dog," *USA Today*, September 24, 2014, https://www.usatoday.com/story/news/nation-now/2014/09/23/humane-society-investigation-kohls-real-fur-coat/16101279/.

7 Emily Slawek, "There is now a $2,145 version of the iconic blue Ikea tote," *TODAY*, April 17, 2017, http://www.today.com/style/balenciaga-s-arena-tote-2-145-version-ikea-bag-t110397.

8 Tom McAllister, "A Space Ripe for Experimentation: The Future of Print Literary Journals," *The Millions*, May 18, 2017, http://www.themillions.com/2017/05/a-space-ripe-for-experimentation-the-future-of-print-literary-journals.html.

Chapter 3

1 "Homo sapiens " in "What does it mean to be human?" Smithsonian National Museum of Natural History, http://humanorigins.si.edu/evidence/human-fossils/species/homo-sapiens (accessed August 26, 2017).

2 Mary Elizabeth Massey, *Ersatz in the Confederacy: Shortages and Substitutes on the Southern Homefront* (Columbia: University of South Carolina Press, 1993), 31.

3 A. C. Gordon, "Hard Times in the Confederacy," *Century Magazine* XXXVI (1888): 762.

4 *Confederate receipt book. A compilation of over one hundred receipts, adapted to the times*, 7–8, https://ia802702.us.archive.org/27/items/confederaterecei00rich/confederaterecei00rich.pdf.

5 *Confederate*, 7.

6 Cameron C. Nickels, *Civil War Humor* (Jackson: University Press of Mississippi, 2010), 62–63.

7 "Patriotism Now Gauged by Bread," *Evening Herald*, May 10, 1918, http://chroniclingamerica.loc.gov/lccn/sn99063812/1918-05-10/ed-1/seq-1/ (accessed August 26, 2017).

8 Massey, *Ersatz*, 65.

9 Ibid., 66.

10 "Okra—A Substitute for Coffee," *Southern Banner*, February 11, 1863, http://georgiainfo.galileo.usg.edu/thisday/cwhistory/02/11/okra-offered-as-substitute-for-coffee (accessed August 26, 2017).

11 "Substitutes for Coffee," *Southern Banner*, March 15, 1865, https://civilwartalk.com/threads/confederate-coffee-substitutes.74380/ (accessed August 26, 2017).

12 Gregory Fremont-Barnes, *Nelson's Sailors* (Oxford, UK: Osprey Publishing, 2005), 24.

13 Massey, *Ersatz*, 73.

14 Mark Pendergrast, *Uncommon Grounds: The History of Coffee and How It Transformed Our World* (New York: Basic Books, 2010), 46.

15 *Confederate*, 17.

16 "Stick Right To It," *Akron Daily Democrat*, March 30, 1901, http://chroniclingamerica.loc.gov/lccn/sn84028140/1901-03-30/ed-1/seq-1/ (accessed August 26, 2017).

17 "Opens His Eyes," *Sacramento Record-Union*, November 25, 1897, http://chroniclingamerica.loc.gov/lccn/sn82015104/1897-11-25/ed-1/seq-4/ (accessed August 26, 2017).

18 Ibid.

19 Samuel Hopkins Adams, *The Great American Fraud* (Chicago: P. F. Collier, 1906), 9.

20 Adams, *Fraud*, 10.

21 Ibid., 55.

22 Pendergrast, *Uncommon Grounds*, 101.

23 "The 'Yell-Oh' Man And One of His Ways," *Guthrie Daily Leader*, September 6, 1907, http://chroniclingamerica.loc.gov/lccn/sn86063952/1907-09-06/ed-1/seq-3/ (accessed August 26, 2017).

24 "'Boo-hoo' Shouts a Spanked Baby," *Citizen-Republican*, October 17, 1907, http://chroniclingamerica.loc.gov/lccn/sn99062010/1907-10-17/ed-1/seq-3/ (accessed August 26, 2017).

25 Mahita Gajanan, "So Your Store-bought Parmesan Cheese is Made with Wood Pulp. Is that so Bad?" *Guardian*, February 17, 2016, https://www.theguardian.com/lifeandstyle/2016/feb/17/parmesan-cheese-store-bought-wood-pulp.

Chapter 4

1 Ada Louise Huxtable, *The Unreal America: Architecture and Illusion* (New York: The New Press, 1997), 107.

2 Huxtable, *Unreal*, 164.

3 Ibid., 134.

4 Ibid., 146.

5 Ibid., 88.

6 Ibid., 116.

7 Jean Baudrillard, *Simulation and Simulacra*, trans. Sheila Faria Glaser (Ann Arbor: University of Michigan Press, 1994), 9.

8 Allan Needell, email to author, July 25, 2017.

9 Huxtable, *Unreal*, 84.

10 Ariel Sabar, "When Collectors Cut Off Pieces of the Star-Spangled Banner As Keepsakes," *Smithsonian Magazine*, June 2014, http://www.smithsonianmag.com/history/when-collectors-cut-off-pieces-star-spangled-banner-keepsakes-180951436/.

11 Huxtable, *Unreal*, 86.

12 Ibid., 179.

Chapter 5

1 Paul Kerley, "The Dentures Made from the Teeth of Dead Soldiers at Waterloo," *BBC News Magazine*, June 16, 2015, http://www.bbc.com/news/magazine-33085031.

2 Matthew Bennett, "War and Technology Gallery," *BBC History*, February 17, 2011, http://www.bbc.co.uk/history/worldwars/war_tech_gallery_04.shtml.

3 Edgar Allan Poe, "The Man That was Used Up" (1850), http://
   xroads.virginia.edu/~hyper/poe/used_up.html (accessed
   August 26, 2017).

4 Veterans Health Administration, "'I was a one-sided person':
   THE DEKA Arm, a VA Research partnership with DoD,"
   https://www.youtube.com/watch?v=KCUwoxuAdYQ&feature
   =youtu.be.

5 Pamela Gallagher, "Development and psychometric
   evaluation of the Trinity Amputation and Prosthesis
   Experience Scales (TAPES)," *Rehabilitation Psychology* 45, no.
   2 (May 2000): 140.

6 "Limb Loss Statistics," *Amputee Coalition*, http://www.
   amputee-coalition.org/limb-loss-resource-center/resources-
   by-topic/limb-loss-statistics/limb-loss-statistics/#.WSY1-
   8a1s2w (accessed August 26, 2017).

7 Dr. Justin Sanchez, "Revolutionizing Prosthetics," *DARPA*,
   http://www.darpa.mil/program/revolutionizing-prosthetics
   (accessed August 26, 2017).

8 Bruce Rybarczyk et al., "Body Image, Perceived Social Stigma,
   and the Prediction of Psychosocial Adjustment to Leg
   Amputation," *Rehabilitation Psychology* (June 1995): 103.

9 Jean Baudrillard, *Simulation and Simulacra*, trans. Sheila Faria
   Glaser (Ann Arbor: University of Michigan Press, 1994), 100.

10 Vivian Sobchack, "A Leg To Stand On: Prosthetics, Metaphor,
   and Materiality," in *The Prosthetic Impulse: From A Posthuman
   Present To A Biocultural Future*, ed. Marquard Smith and
   Joanne Morra (Cambridge, MA: MIT Press, 2006), 27.

11 Sobchack, "Leg," 17–18.

12 Donna Haraway, "A Cyborg Manifesto," in *The Cybercultures
   Reader*, ed. David Bell and Barbara M. Kennedy (London:
   Routledge, 2000), 313.

13 Nicolas Salazar Sutil, "Intelligence Behind Movement: Laboratories of Biomechanics and the Making of Movement Utopia," in *Digital Movement: Essays in Motion Technology and Performance*, ed. Sutil and Sita Popit (New York: Palgrave Macmillan, 2015), 46.

14 Nikolay Chernyshevsky, *What is to Be Done?* trans. Michael R. Katz (Ithaca, NY: Cornell University Press, 1989), 181.

Chapter 6

1 "Criminal impersonation in the first degree," Penal Law—PEN § 190.26, New York Consolidated Laws.

2 Huxtable, *Unreal*, 122.

3 "Details of hybrid clone revealed," *BBC News*, June 18, 1999, http://news.bbc.co.uk/2/hi/science/nature/371378.stm.

4 Haraway, "Cyborg," 293–94.

5 Ibid., 314.

Chapter 7

1 Timothy L. Taylor, *The Prehistory of Sex: Four Million Years of Human Sexual Culture* (New York: Bantam, 1996), 128.

2 Aziz Ansari, *Modern Romance* (New York: Penguin, 2015), 166.

3 Ovid, *The Love Books of Ovid Being the Amores, Ars Amatoria, Remedia Amoris and Medicamina Faciei Femineae of Publius Ovidius Naso*, trans. J. Lewis May (Whitefish, MT: Kessinger, 2005), http://www.sacred-texts.com/cla/ovid/lboo/lboo60.htm.

4 Ovid, http://www.sacred-texts.com/cla/ovid/lboo/lboo59.htm.

5 Taylor, *Prehistory*, 43.

Chapter 8

1 Jaruwan Sakuluku, "The Impostor Phenomenon," *International Journal of Behavioral Science* 6, no. 1 (2011): 73–92.

INDEX